SEX AND
SUPERVISION

Recent Titles in
Contributions in Criminology and Penology

Sex and Supervision

GUARDING MALE AND FEMALE INMATES

Joycelyn M. Pollock

FOREWORD BY
Elaine A. Lord

CONTRIBUTIONS IN CRIMINOLOGY AND PENOLOGY, NUMBER 12

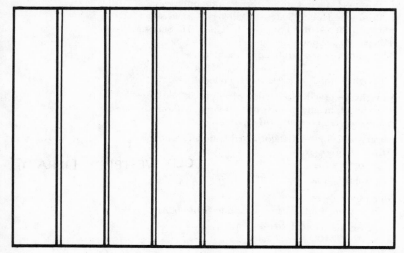

Greenwood Press
NEW YORK
WESTPORT, CONNECTICUT
LONDON

Library of Congress Cataloging-in-Publication Data

Pollock, Joycelyn M., 1956–
  Sex and supervision.

  (Contributions in criminology and penology,
ISSN 0732-4464; no. 12)
  Bibliography: p.
  Includes index.
    1. Women correctional personnel–United States.
  2. Prisons–United States–Officials and employees.
  3. Prisoners–United States–Psychology. 4. Prison
  administration–United States. I. Title. II. Series.
  HV9470.P65 1986   365'.6   86-9987
  ISBN 0-313-25410-9 (lib. bdg.: alk. paper)

Library of Congress Catalog Card Number: 86-9987
ISBN: 0-313-25410-9
ISSN: 0732-4464

First published in 1986

Greenwood Press, Inc.
88 Post Road West, Westport, Connecticut 06881

Printed in the United States of America

The paper used in this book complies with the
Permanent Paper Standard issued by the National
Information Standards Organization (Z39.48-1984).

10 9 8 7 6 5 4 3 2 1

To Hans Toch

Contents

Tables

Foreword

When I first entered Corrections as a custodial officer in a juvenile training school, supervision strictly reflected the sex of the charges. In the boys' cottages, the custodial staff were males, while in the girls' cottage the custodial staff were females. However, the women custodial officers were not expected to deal with "serious" incidents such as fights. In these instances, setting off an alarm was both a call for assistance and a signal which precipitated pandemonium among the girls in residence. They would immediately begin running up and down the halls screaming, "The men are coming, the men are coming. Look out, look out, they'll have clubs." Thus, a fight usually became an all-out disturbance with girls running in all directions, the more experienced ones communicating their agitation to the younger or newer girls.

It was in this manner that the institution responded to calm situations and regain control, and the same was true in most female correctional institutions throughout the country until the 1970s. To me, this situation was the most surreal experience of my initiation into Corrections. Female staff were simply not expected to deal with certain situations, but were to remain "ladylike." As a result, their female charges interacted with males only in instances laden with potential violence or the use of force. When situations got out of hand, the men arrived to restore order by whatever means necessary. I always wondered just what kind of a message about the roles of males and females this response communicated to the girls incarcerated there.

Even in the institution that I presently run, history is not much different. Until the mid 1970s, the correctional officer staff were females, with the exception of a few "safety" officers who were located on the outside perimeter. I still remember on one of my first trips to the institution, asking about an older male sitting in a chair outside the fence. It was explained to me that he was stationed there and responded in the event of a fight or disturbance. Adult women felons rather than delinquent girls—but still the same mode of operation and an identical method of supervision. The inmates who have been here long enough make me aware that they too, ran around hollering, "The men are coming, the men are coming."

Today, all that has changed. Court cases relating to equal employment opportunities have opened male institutions to women correctional officers, and female institutions to male correctional officers. At this facility, the State's maximum security facility for women, approximately 60 percent of the officer staff is female, and 40 percent male. The women inmates countersued that the abundance of males violated their right to privacy, but the result was a morass of compromises that provided them privacy curtains for their doors, one-piece pajamas if they so desired, and "female only" posts in the hospital, and at least one female on outside trips. The present situation is not really satisfactory to facility administrators, female or male correctional officers, or inmates. Litigation is bound to continue for some years to come, not only in this jurisdiction, but as an equitable solution to conflicting needs is sought.

Yet, in spite of the problems of operating a women's institution with male correction officers staffing housing units, or the need to juggle for a female escort, I personally would not want to go back. I believe that male correctional officers have a valid role to play within a women's prison, and that women correctional officers also have a valid and important place in prisons for men.

Prisons are truly worlds in and of themselves, but to try to keep them one-dimensional in our very complicated society seems inappropriate. A well-managed prison should have room for different styles of supervision whether by male or female officers, just as not all inmates are the same, whether male or female. Males and females are socialized differently in our society and they bring these differences in perception and action to prison, whether as inmates or correctional officers.

I would suggest that both women inmates and women officers tend to react more emotionally because their socialization in this society allows such reactions on the part of women. Female inmates write many letters to facility staff, voicing both complaints and appreciation, as they see fit. Female staff also appear to follow similar modes of behavior in terms of administrators. Thus, I would suggest simply that expression of emotion is more acceptable to women. It is simply a part of the way they react to the world. I am not suggesting that emotions override rationality, but rather that women interpret and perceive the world through emotions and through their relations with others.

To put it simply, men and women are different. They are raised differently and have a different view of the world. These perceptions carry over, whether they find themselves administrators, officers or inmates. I would agree, as the research in this book suggests, that female inmates focus on small groups of intimates, while males focus on larger, less intimate social groupings. This is a function of their basically different ways of perceiving the world. This perception also translates to differences in supervision styles by both male and female officers. Women staff tend to be more open to inmate problems, while male staff tend to be more organizationally oriented and tend to slide into the paramilitary and authoritarian role of the officer more easily. However, as the book suggests, officers do tend to make adjustments in style of supervision to fit their setting. These differences, of course, also vary a great deal within individuals.

Part of what may be needed is a simple, unapologetic acknowledgment that women are women, not men. They worry about relationships, about family. Indeed, one of the problems which seems to be propelling more women into correction officer jobs is the significant wage increase they experience. On the inmate side, women appear to maintain their role as mothers despite the role of the prison in separating inmates from their communities. Thus, staff in a female prison are used to and expect to hear from concerned family members with some frequency, and indeed, find themselves passing on a message because mother is needed to make a decision with regard to her child.

Yet, what is appropriate for a female officer toward a female inmate would not be appropriate for a male and, conversely, what is appropriate for a male officer dealing with male inmates is not necessarily appropriate for a female dealing with male inmates. This book explores some of these differences by addressing the perceptions of both male and female officers working with male and female inmates. This will remain a complex and controversial area for some years to come. Training can and should be developed to help guide new staff in dealing with a variety of situations. Corrections needs to be less caught up with keeping all inmates at arms length and rather, needs to become more sophisticated in identifying what works best in different situations. This could help to increase job satisfaction and lessen work-related stress, as well as help us to move beyond simplistic sexual stereotypes of males and females, whether as clients or workers.

Elaine A. Lord

Preface

The research reported in this book was conducted under the auspices of the School of Criminal Justice, State University of New York at Albany. The research effort was funded by a $500 grant from the SUNY Benevolent Association.

A decision was made to keep the identity of the state private; unfortunately, this prevents a public acknowledgment of the cooperation and assistance received from many people. The central office staff gave permission for the study and helped identify the sample group. The administration and supervisory staff at the facilities were extremely cooperative in agreeing to be interviewed themselves and/or setting up the officer interviews. This was often done at great inconvenience to themselves since each officer interviewed was taken from a post which had to be filled by a relief officer.

I would also like to thank Hans Toch, SUNY–Albany; William Brigman, University of Houston–Downtown; and Antony P. Byrne for reading earlier drafts or parts of this book. A special note of thanks goes to Robert Fisher, University of Houston–Downtown, who was instrumental in getting the book published.

Naturally, without the willingness of the officers and other correctional staff, there would have been no results at all. The enthusiasm, insight, and dedication most officers hold for their profession made the interviewing phase of this research enjoyable as well as enlightening.

SEX AND
SUPERVISION

1

Guards

A cursory glance at correctional literature will show that correctional officers have only recently drawn the attention of researchers. Long ignored in studies of prisoners and prison subcultures, correctional officers are now recognized as integral participants in the prison world. In the past, correctional officers were viewed as one-dimensional cartoon characters, as brutal ignorant louts preying on prisoner victims. They have now been recognized as complex human actors with perceptions, values, and skills worthy of study. In this first chapter we will briefly explore some of the recent research on correctional officers, including research on female correctional officers and their entry into prisons for men.

NATURE OF JOB

In most states correctional officers tend to be white males. Salary levels range from $6,000 a year (starting salary) to $25,000 a year (with overtime and seniority).[1] Turnover tends to be very high, and various reasons are given for this. Jacobs and Grear found that lack of safety, family responsibilities, working conditions, superior officers, and lack of opportunity for promotion were some of the reasons cited by officers who had quit.[2] There is often a lack of training, especially in states that are belatedly trying to increase staff to meet court-mandated officer-inmate ratios.[3] Crouch and Marquart report that officers often do not plan on correctional careers, but rather drift into corrections because of other reasons, such as layoffs or retirement.[4]

There are several studies on certain aspects of the occupation, such as victimization. From all accounts, it seems that the ever-present fear and knowledge of the potential for victimization are more relevant than actual victimization.[5] Some statistics, however, indicate that officers may be more likely to be assaulted today than they ever have been in the past.[6]

Another topic which has gained a great deal of attention lately is job-related stress and ways to alleviate it. It appears that officers experience stress differentially, depending on type of institution, education, and other factors.[7] Cullen and others indicate that stress is multifaceted, including the distinct concepts of work stress, job satisfaction, and life stress. They found that role problems and perceived dangerousness affected job stress, while supervisory support mitigated stress and job dissatisfaction. Blacks and educated officers experienced more job dissatisfaction in this sample, and female officers exhibited more work stress. Interestingly, relations with peers seemed to be positively correlated with stress in this study.[8] This is somewhat contradictory to the hypothesis that a strong guard subculture insulates and supports the officer in the prison environment.

Articles on screening, training, and evaluating officers indicate that this occupation is now being considered worthy of professional attention.[9] For instance, Hawkins discusses officer selection and the various tools that could be used to hire competent people.[10] Several states are either preparing to use or are actually using psychological testing in addition to physical agility tests for hiring applicants.

Socialization

Socialization into the guard subculture is another growing area of research interest. It is believed by some that there is a strong officer subculture because of the nature of the job. "The stigmatization of the job, the peculiar working hours, and the frequent isolation of the prisons in out of the way places make for a certain esprit and solidarity among the guards."[11] Thus, we see a similar argument as that used to explain the origin of the prisoner subculture. Interestingly, both of these subcultures have come under scrutiny recently and been found to have less relevance for the individual than what was thought at first.[12]

If a guard subculture is relevant at all, it is for socialization of new officers. Several descriptions are available of the process in which new officers learn how to deal with inmates in the prison environment. Typically, instructions include admonitions to stay away from inmates and not become overly friendly with them. This rule is formalized in some states, and an offending officer could get officially sanctioned. "If you stopped and talked to a convict for more than one or two minutes, you were being watched. And someone would write you a pinky."[13] The reasons for this caution stem from the reciprocity and corruption Sykes describes in *Society of Captives*.[14] Research indicates that careless officers are still bound to inmates by "favors" in payment for keeping a tier under control, completing an assignment, or overlooking an officer transgression.[15]

Crouch and Marquart provide officer explanations for the need to act "tough" in interactions with inmates. Using obscene language and conveying orders in loud tones are not only habit, but they are believed to be the most effective way to reach inmates. Officers may even mask confusion or ignorance over certain policies and rules by a harsh bravado towards inmates. They summarize the guard socialization process as one characterized by cynicism and authoritarianism.[16]

This does not mean, however, that there is an explicit or even implicit "war" between officers and inmates. Some writers describe an almost jocular interaction between male officers and male inmates, with at least superficial acceptance and some isolated relationships based on respect and friendship. However, "such relations are typically superficial and are tolerated only so long as the dominance of the guard is not questioned."[17] There are places in the prison where fairly positive relationships between officers and inmates do occur, such as the workshop or other areas where the officer and inmate are involved in a neutral activity over a long period of time.[18] Other writers describe close to kinship relations between some officers and inmates, even including the use of terms like "kid" and "dad" or "daddy;" not in a sexual sense, as is the case in the prisoner subculture, but rather to denote a paternalistic relationship.[19]

The question whether certain "types" (individuals possessing certain characteristics) are drawn to correctional work, or whether the nature of the prison itself changes the officer is long-standing. Many individuals quote the Zimbardo or Stanford experiment as evidence that it is the possession of power that corrupts otherwise normal people into abusers of power. Unfortunately, we do not have the research to answer these questions. Kercher and Martin found that attitudes towards prisoners and the job change over time in a U-shaped curve. Early in their career, officers are fairly punitive and go "by the book" with inmates; gradually they lose their rigidity, and then later in their careers, they regain some of these attitudes.[20] Other studies find that the attitude scales in use may be misleading and hide some aspects of officer interaction and attitudes towards inmates. For instance, according to another researcher, it may be that officers become more stern with inmates in their interactions but have less punitive attitudes towards inmates in general and their need for "punishment."[21]

Another study has shown that attitudes toward inmates are somewhat correlated with the type of institution. Not surprisingly, officers in maximum security institutions display the most punitive attitudes (having a "punishment orientation"); while those in less secure environments were more likely to possess a "work ethic" in place of a punishment orientation. Also, in this same study, it was found that education was related to less punitive attitudes.[22] Interestingly, studies indicate that race and sex may not affect attitudes since black officers and female officers seem to exhibit attitudes about inmates similar to those of white males.[23]

Officer typologies are another way to describe individual adaptational patterns to the correctional officer role. Crouch and Marquart discuss officer types in terms of success or failure in assuming the guard role: the "limited failure" and the "ritualist" are only marginally successful, while the "successful officer" and the "insider" have comfortably mastered their environment.[24] Smith lists four types and describes how an officer tends to go through stages upon entry into the officer role. All entry officers tend to "go by the book" at first, and then some move to other stages such as "coopted," "firm but fair," or "tuned out."[25] Crouch also describes two types of supervision in a Southern prison dependent on whether the officer supervised field crews ("by the boot") or building staff ("by the book").[26]

The most interesting type of officer is described by Johnson and called the "human service officer." This officer is concerned with inmate problems and develops informal helping networks with treatment staff. Johnson postulates that about one in every five correction officers (C.O.s) combine custodial with human service obligations.[27] This is interesting for our purposes because the "human service officer" possesses many of the qualities that are said to characterize the female correctional officer, that is, a helping, more service-oriented attitude towards inmates.

FEMALES

The entry of women into corrections parallels their entry into the police profession. Both have a long history in each of these subsystems of criminal justice but only recently have challenged their separate status and role. Both are still represented by small numbers, especially in administrative positions. Both attained their current position only by court challenge and struggle against strong male resistance. Finally, in both areas, there is evidence that women, with only a few exceptions, succeed as well as men in the performance of their role.

The earliest women hired by police departments were given special roles based on the perceived skills of their sex, such as supervising women in jails as matrons and assistance with juvenile cases. In the early 1900s Alice Stebbins Wells started the first women's bureau in the Los Angeles Police Department. The role of this bureau combined social work and police work.[28] During both world wars women were hired in greater numbers and given larger roles, only to be laid off or relegated to minor roles after the manpower shortage ended. Most departments had special quota systems and different hiring standards for women. For instance, college degrees were required for women, but male applicants needed only a high school diploma.[29] It wasn't until the 1960s that women challenged this differential treatment.

Title VII of the Civil Rights Act was used in a challenge by a woman officer who demanded the right to take a sergeant's exam. This case was followed by others that challenged methods of testing height and weight restrictions for hiring. In 1968 Indianapolis put women out on patrol and the year after that, Washington, D.C., integrated its patrol force. It was here that the first in-depth evaluation of policewomen was carried out.[30]

Evaluations such as the D.C. study found that women made fewer arrests but were more likely to make "good" arrests. They were less likely than men to engage in behavior unbecoming to an officer or get complaints from the public. Women tended to have slightly more difficulty learning firearm and driving skills, but there were no differences found in number of sick days taken, tendency to give or receive instructions, frequency in the use of backups, or departmental ratings.[31]

Another evaluation of the same integration found that women who had already been employed by the department and had entered the profession without expectations of patrol work were somewhat bitter and unable to adapt to the assignments. This author found that women, more so than men, tended to drift into police work from other professions. They entered police work with less anticipatory socialization; that is, they had less experience with aggression in organized sports, teamwork, or authority. Women had to learn new patterns of behavior, such as developing an authoritative tone, learning new facial expressions (not to smile as much), and using more direct language to convey directives. Women adapted to these new demands by assuming one of several role types; such as the "little sister," "sexual flirt," or "mother" figure.[32] In one analysis, women who embraced the police role and competed with men were called POLICEwomen by the author, while the other types were combined under a role of policeWOMEN, indicating the master role of the individual.[33]

Other evaluations of policewomen show that in academies, there are no differences in academic or technical measures, but there are significant differences in defensive tactics skills.[34] An evaluation in Detroit found no differences in number of suspensions, injury days or merit days off, and number of arrests or citizen complaints. Women, however, took more sick days and males had more commendations.[35] Another study found that women made fewer arrests, but all other measures were comparable. This author described the women's style of policing as less aggressive than the men's, and citizens perceived women to be more sensitive and responsive.[36]

Most studies find that male officers and administrators have varying negative reactions to the entry of female officers, although some factors, such as education and age, can affect their attitudes positively.[37] Primarily, men fear women cannot handle themselves in violent confrontations or situations where strength or physical agility is necessary. This male resistance leads to women's exclusion from the police subculture. Authors discuss the incompatibility of the feminine stereotype with the male-oriented subculture associated with police work, i.e., the concepts of danger, excitement, and power.[38]

There is no doubt that women, especially the first women who entered patrol work, had to deal with sex-role stereotype conflicts. Because the police role is fairly inconsistent with the traditional feminine role, women who perform police work are perceived as less feminine. One study found that despite their behavior, women officers were perceived as more assertive than male officers. Demanding female officers were seen as less feminine than "reasoning" female police officers. Also, challenging a female officer was seen as more legitimate than challenging a male officer.[39]

Policewomen's role conflict has been associated with job-related stress by more than one researcher. The difficulty in interacting with male officers has already been noted. Women must walk a fine line between appearing too friendly and too aloof towards male peers. This is difficult to adjust to for many. It also appears that women have a difficult time acting "out of character" during the performance of the police role and then, after work, reverting to traditional feminine behavior. For instance, women officers report that they have a tendency to become extremely authoritarian towards family members as a natural carryover from their behavior on the street.[40]

Despite these findings, personal accounts from female police

officers indicate that they have little difficulty with public interactions. Examples show that female police officers using per-
suasion can achieve the same results as male officers with no use
of force or violence.[41] Thus, there is evidence that women police
officers generally do not totally adopt male behavior patterns,
but rather adapt their personal characteristics to the job at hand.
Some studies indicate that women not only use "feminine traits"
in their interactions with the public, but also serve a nurturing,
confidante role with fellow officers. In one study female officers
explained that male officers felt comfortable discussing problems
with them: "We policewomen are like a crying towel," and "Yes,
the policemen do seem to open up more to a woman."[42]

Corrections

As with the police, women have been a part of corrections
almost from its inception. However, their early role was also
relegated to tasks reflective of their sex, primarily guarding female inmates. In the mid–1800s a number of reform groups
protested the use of men to supervise female inmates. They
believed that women of upstanding character would be better
suited to teach and serve as role models for the misguided woman
dealt with in corrections. In 1873 the first separate institution
for women was built in Indiana and this facility, as did all others,
incorporated special architectural and policy features thought
to be suited to the clientele. Security was less emphasized than
a homelike atmosphere. Staff lived on the premises and were
required to be single, virtuous, and able to handle their charges
in a "ladylike manner."[43]

It wasn't until the 1970s that women correctional officers were
placed in prisons for men. Their first tasks were solely to search
female visitors and carry out administration building duties.
Gradually, states started to use woman for more varied tasks in
prisons for men, including staffing posts within the living units.
These states, such as New York, had policies prohibiting women
from strip searches, shower supervision, or escort duty outside
the prison. There had to be at least one C.O. of the same sex
on the living unit at all times, the opposite-sex C.O. announced

their presence on the tier, and females could not exceed one-third of the force.[44]

The courts have played a significant role in the attempt to enlarge the role of females in corrections. *Dothard v. Rawlinson*, a case involving a woman who demanded to work in an Alabama prison, was a setback for women since the Supreme Court held that because of the circumstances of Alabama's maximum security prison, women could be excluded from posts within it. Specifically, the Court was apprehensive about well-documented brutal conditions; in fact, the entire Alabama system was already under a Court mandate because of the violence and unconstitutional conditions present. However, the Court's decision did not categorically bar women from other prisons.[45]

Subsequently, in *Gunther v. Iowa* a federal district court held that privacy rights of inmates should not take precedence over a female correctional officer's right to promotion, and the administration of the prison should make arrangements to allow them in without compromising inmates' privacy.[46]

Today many states have women in male institutions and men in female institutions; not without some problems, however. New York reports problems with bidding systems (since women are placed at posts sought after by senior officers). There are several lawsuits pending, and the extent of women's activity in prisons for men will be in contention for some time to come.[47]

In the meantime, evaluations are appearing on women correctional officers' performances in prisons and jails for men. There are still problems with full participation; administrators do not assign them to certain posts (because of either individual bias or policy); women are told to stay away from emergency situations; and they encounter hostility and resentment from male officers.[48] However, some studies indicate that male officers who are young and have more education possess less negative attitudes toward women officers, even to the point of saying they "improved" the prison.[49]

Kissel and Seidel's study of female officers in several jails indicates that women were perceived to be competent in giving first aid, cooling down angry inmates, dealing with verbally abusive inmates, and controlling mentally or emotionally disturbed inmates. They were perceived as less competent in separating two fighting inmates and controlling big and tough inmates. This study found that the majority of men and women officers said they got along "equally well" with both sexes. Males did perceive women as needing more help (56 percent) and were less likely to rate females' help as excellent or good. Especially in violent or potentially violent situations, male help was more appreciated (71 percent of men preferred men; 53 percent of women preferred men). This study found that inmates may react to the presence of females by taking greater care with their appearance, toning down their language, and generally behaving in a more polite and respectful manner towards female officers than male officers. Three out of four male officers and 80 percent of inmates gave females favorable ratings.[50]

Similar to policewomen, females in corrections entered by different paths than men. Women are less likely than men to list corrections as a career goal; rather, they chose corrections because of financial reasons or because the job was close to home.[51] A general survey of women in corrections found that women still tended to be concentrated in clerical or support-staff positions. They were more likely than males to cite salary considerations as reasons for entering corrections. They seem to have lower career aspirations than men, lower job satisfaction, and less positive attitudes towards employee relations.[52]

Similar to studies of policewomen, research shows that women experience a great deal of role strain when entering correctional work. They encounter harassment and hostility from some male officers and some inmates. Women adapt to role expectations by adopting role types paralleling those described in female police work, i.e., one in which the female tries to outdo the male, and another modified role where her "feminine" traits are retained in a special role in the correctional environment (such as "little sister" or "mother").[53]

Most evidence indicates that women in male prisons perform the role of the C.O. job somewhat differently from males. There are examples of women adopting a more service-oriented role than male officers, and a less aggressive style of supervising.[54] Obviously, this is very consistent with the behavior of women in the police field.

It should be noted that these findings are not inconsistent with published data from studies of females in other professions. Women are perceived to have different skills, different habits, and different motivations from males. These differences also make them perceived as less desirable workers. Partly because of these perceived differences, women have remained within a small number of occupations and even within a typically male profession, have congregated in female specialties.

Professions which employ large numbers of women have been called "semiprofessions" and the "occupational ghetto"—these include social work, nursing, elementary school teaching, and so on. Also, a tipping function is said to occur when too many women enter a male profession wherein the whole profession is downgraded in status.[55] When women do comprise large numbers in a work force, it is believed that this has a definite impact on the nature of the organization, specifically, the organization becomes more centralized with less autonomy for the worker and more power concentrated in a few top positions. This is thought to occur because of the psychological characteristics of women workers, including a greater deference to authority, greater need for approval and association, guilt about expressing aggressiveness, and less opposition to centralization because of less commitment to the job and less concern with decision making. Other reasons are structural—women workers have been shown to have more absenteeism and turnover, necessitating centralized authority.[56]

Another study disputes this last hypothesis, finding that absenteeism and turnover between men and women are very similar and, further, that job orientation and work motivation are similar, at least among college students. The author proposed the idea that an intervening variable of professionalism might affect the prevalence of centralization in organizations composed of women workers. The author hypothesizes that professionals are less likely to be organized in a centralized fashion, and since professional organizations are likely to be male, it is not the sex difference but the nature of the work which affects centralization.[57]

Recent findings show that female workers are similar to male workers in terms of job satisfactions and motivations. For example, one author rejects the idea that the woman worker is not interested in the intrinsic aspects of her job and cannot be influenced by job enrichment; "women who do substantively complex or non-routine work tend to be more intellectually flexible, to take more personal responsibility for moral standards and to be more receptive to innovation and change."[58]

Two concepts present in the literature on women workers which relate to female correctional workers are supervision and the nurturant role attributed to women. Wolf and Fligstein explored the reasons why women are not found in authority positions in other professions. They looked at three possible factors: (1) the woman's qualifications; (2) the behavior and policies of the employers; and (3) the activities of the women themselves. They concluded that the behavior of the employers in excluding women from authority roles was far more determinant than the other two factors.[59]

Two studies examining supervisory styles obtained interesting findings. The first used students who evaluated scenarios of three supervisory styles: directive, rational, and friendly. The friendly style was rated as most satisfactory for both sexes, but the directive style when performed by a woman was rated even less favorably than when performed by a man.[60]

The second study used banking executives who rated supervisory styles labeled unemotional-calm and emotional-angry. This group rated the unemotional-calm style more satisfactory, but the emotional reaction obtained less negative scores when performed by a woman.[61] In effect, emotional supervision seems to be more acceptable for women than a directive style.

The second concept involves the widely approved nurturant role of women and its predominance in the workplace. We are all familiar with the nurturant role assigned to women in the family. While the male has been perceived as providing material support to the family, the female's role has been to provide emotional support.[62] Several studies indicate this role is carried over into the workplace.

Perhaps the most common component of all roles women perform is what Bernard calls women's "stroking" function. This function characterizes the universally supportive role women are supposed to take. Many roles considered appropriate for women, both in the family and in the world of work, are characterized by their supportive, enabling, facilitating, and vicarious features.[63]

There is support for the belief that this role supplants the supervisory role of women in positions of power since a woman's authority has traditionally been tied primarily to her position as mother:

The presence of a female leader in a work group appears to stimulate unusually strong dependency needs within the group and to lead directly to the formation of a basic assumption of dependency. That is, the staff is likely to unconsciously perceive the female leader's task as feeding and training, no matter what task has been designated to her in reality. Members of the group thereupon present themselves as though they were helpless children eager to be fed and taught.[64]

The role is also played out by the woman herself. For example, female therapists differed significantly from male therapists in their patterns of goal behavior: "A greater proportion of female therapists endorsed supportive type goals than male therapists, who ... were either high on insight oriented goals alone, or were low on all three goal clusters."[65]

In summary, there seems to be evidence that although female workers are similar to male workers in job achievement and work patterns, they may be perceived differently. Also, they might be different in supervisory styles and conceptions of their role within an occupation. This seems to be supported by the police and correctional literature cited above. These findings are important for us since we will be looking at differences in female and male perceptions of inmates and role demands in interactions with male and female inmates.

NOTES

1. E. May, "Prison Guards in America: The Inside Story," in *The Keepers: Prison Guards and Contemporary Corrections*, ed. B. Crouch (Springfield, IL: Charles C. Thomas, 1980), p. 115.

2. J. Jacobs and M. Grear, "Dropouts and Rejects: An Analysis of the Prison Guard's Revolving Door," in *The Keepers*, p. 286.

3. May, "Prison Guards in America," p. 130.

4. B. Crouch and J. Marquart, "On Becoming a Prison Guard," in *The Keepers*, p. 65.

5. J. Jacobs and H. Retsky, "Prison Guard," in *The Keepers*, pp. 183–206; also L. Bowker, *Prison Victimization*, (New York: Elsevier, 1980).

6. D. Fuller and T. Orsagh, "Violence and Victimization within a State Prison System," *Criminal Justice Review*, 2, no. 2 (1977); 35–56.

7. Articles dealing with correctional officer stress include F. Cheek and M.Miller, "Reducing Staff and Inmate Stress," *Corrections Today* 44, no. 5 (1982): 72–76; F. Cheek and M. Miller, "The Experience of Stress for C.O.'s: A Double Bind Theory of Correctional Stress," *Journal of Criminal Justice*, II, no. 2 (1983): 105–112; C. Brodsky, "Long Term Work Stress in Teachers and Prison Guards," *Journal of Occupational Medicine* 19 (1977): 133–38; D. Finlay, "Stress: An Expert's View," *Corrections Today* 45, no. 1 (1983): 58; R. Gardner, "Guard Stress," *Corrections Magazine* 7, no. 5 (1981): 6–10.

8. F. Cullen, B. Link, N. Wolfe and J. Frank, "The Social Dimensions of Correctional Officer Stress," *Justice Quarterly* 2, no. 4 (1985): 505–535.

9. Related articles include: D. Camp, "Mandated Correctional Training: A Task Analysis Approach to Curriculum Design," Paper presented at Academy of Criminal Justice Sciences Conference, Las Vegas, Nevada, 1985; J. Stinchcomb, "Why Not the Best?: Using Assessment Centers for Officer Selection," *Corrections Today* 47, no. 3 (June 1985): 120–24; H. Cavallin, "The Case Study: A Clinical Approach to the Training of the Correctional Officer," *American Journal of Corrections* 29 (1967): 14–18; Y. Cohn, "Toward Job-Related Inservice Training in Corrections," *Federal Probation* 44 (June 1980): 48–57; J. Cohen, "Correctional Academy: Emergence of a New Institution," *Crime and Delinquency* 25, no. 2 (1979): 177–99; R. Downey and E. I. Signori, "The Selection of Prison Guards," *Journal of Criminal Law; Criminology and Police Science* 49 (1958): 234–36; M. J. Gilbert, "Developing Performance Standards for Correctional Officers," *Corrections Today* 42 (1980): 8–9; R. Myren, "Education for Correctional Careers," *Federal Probation* 39, no. 2)1975): 51–58.

10. G. Hawkins, "Correctional Officer Selection and Training," in *The Keepers*, pp. 45–62.

11. Jacobs and Retsky, "Prison Guard," p. 188.

12. J. Klofas and H. Toch, "The Guard Subculture Myth," *Journal of Research in Crime and Delinquency* 19, no. 2 (1982): 258. Also, K. Kaufmann, "Prison Officer Attitudes and Perceptions of Attitudes: A Case of Pluralistic Ignorance," *Journal of Research in Crime and Delinquency* 18, no. 2 (1981): 272–294.

13. May, "Prison Guards in America," p. 120.

14. G. Sykes, *Society of Captives* (Princeton, NJ: Princeton University Press, 1958).

15. For instance, see L. Carroll, *Hacks, Blacks and Cons* (Lexington, MA: Lexington Books, 1974), p. 58.

16. Crouch and Marquart, "On Becoming a Prison Guard," p. 91.

17. Crouch and Marquart, "On Becoming a Prison Guard," p. 87.

18. Jacobs and Retsky, "Prison Guard," p. 195.

19. G. L. Webb and D. G. Morris, "Prison Guard Conceptions," in *The Keepers*, p. 160.

20. As reported in Crouch and Marquart, "On Becoming a Prison Guard," p. 94.

21. Crouch and Marquart, p. 95.

22. P. Maxim and D. Plecas, "Some Factors Influencing the Attitudes of C.O.'s Toward Correctional Policies," Paper presented at Academy of Criminal Justice Sciences Conference, Las Vegas, Nevada, 1985.

23. L. Zupan, "Gender-Related Differences in C.O.'s and Attitudes," Paper presented at Academy of Criminal Justice Sciences Conference, Las Vegas, Nevada, 1985; J. Jacobs and L. J. Kraft, "Integrating the Keepers: A Comparison of Black and White Prison Guards in Illinois," *Social Problems* 25 (1978): 304–318.

24. Crouch and Marquart, "On Becoming a Prison Guard," p. 98.

25. B. Smith, "Styles of Guarding," Paper presented at Academy of Criminal Justice Sciences Conference, Las Vegas, Nevada, 1985.

26. B. Crouch, "The Book v. the Boot: Two Styles of Guarding in a Southern Prison," in *The Keepers*, pp. 207–224.

27. R. Johnson, "Informal Helping Networks: The Shape of Grass Roots Correctional Intervention," in *Prison Guard/Correctional Officer*, ed. R. Ross (Toronto: Butterworths, 1981), p. 106; also, R. Johnson and S. Price, "The Complete Correctional Officer," *Criminal Justice and Behavior* 8, no. 3 (1981): 343–373, and H. Toch, "Is a 'Correctional Officer', By Any Other Name, a 'Screw'?", in *Prison Guard/Correctional Officer*, pp. 87–104.

28. P. Horne, *Women in Law Enforcement* (Springfield, IL: Charles Thomas Publishers, 1975); C. Feinman, *Women in the Criminal Justice System* (New York: Praeger Publishers, 1980).

29. B. Mishkin, "Female Police in the United States," *The Police Journal* 54, no. 1 (1981): 22–23.

30. Mishkin, "Female Police in the United States," p. 22.

31. P. Block and D. Anderson, *Policewomen on Patrol* (Washington, D.C.: Police Foundation, 1974).

32. S. Martin, *Breaking and Entering: Policewomen on Patrol* (Berkeley, CA: University of California Press, 1980).

33. S. Martin, "POLICEwoman and PoliceWOMAN: Occupational Role Dilemmas and Choices of Female Officers," *Journal of Police Science and Administration* 7, no. 3 (1979): 314–23.

34. M. Charles, "The Performance and Socialization of Female Recruits in the Michigan State Police Training Academy," *Journal of Police Science and Administration* 9, no. 2 (1981): 209–223.

35. D. Williams and M. Blumberg, "Female Police Officers: An Empirical Evaluation of Job Performance," Paper presented at Academy of Criminal Justice Sciences Conference, Chicago, 1984.

36. L. Sherman, "Evaluation of Policewomen on Patrol in a Suburban Police Department," *Journal of Police Science and Administration*, 3, no. 4 (1975): 434–38; also see R. Townsey, *National Information and Research Center on Women in Policing. Performance Evaluations—Information Packet* (Rockville, MD: National Institute of Justice, 1980).

37. P. Remmington, *Policing—The Occupation and the Introduction of Female Officers—An Anthropologist's Study* (Lantham, MD: University Press of America, 1981).

38. P. Jacobs, "Female Police Officers: Coping with the Male Police Subculture," Paper presented at Academy of Criminal Justice Conference, Las Vegas, 1985; M. Vega and I. Silverman, "Female Police Officers as Viewed by Their Male Counterparts," *Police Studies* 5, no. 1 (1982): 31–39; and J. McGeorge and J. Wolfe, "Comparison of Attitudes between Men and Women; Police Officers—A Preliminary Analysis," *Criminal Justice Review* 1, no. 2 (1976): 21–33.

39. B. Sterling and J. Owen, "Perceptions of Demanding v. Reasoning Male and Female Police Officers," *Personality and Social Psychology Bulletin* 8, no. 2 (1982): 336–40.

40. J. Wexler and D. Logan, "Sources of Stress among Women Police Officers," *Journal of Police Science and Administration* II, no. 1 (1983): 46–53; and J. Brookshire, "Police Training: A Personal Challenge to the Female Officer," *Police Chief* 47, no. 10 (1980): 258–59.

41. J. Greenwald, "Aggression as a Component of Police-Citizen Transactions—Differences between Male and Female Police Officers," Dissertation, City of New York University, 1976.

42. Jacobs, "Female Police Officers," p. 9.

43. C. Feinman, *Women in the Criminal Justice System*; J. Pollock, "The Female Correctional Officer: Past, Present and Future," Paper presented at American Society of Criminology Conference, Washington, D.C., 1981; and E. Freedman, "Their Sister's Keepers: A Historical Perspective of Female Correctional Institutions in the U.S.," *Feminist Studies*, 2 (1974): 77–95.

44. A. Becker, "Women in Corrections: A Process of Change," *Res-*

olution 1, no. 4 (1975): 19–21; also see F. Coles, "Women in Corrections: Issues and Concerns," in *Improving Management in Criminal Justice*, ed. A. Cohn and B. Ward (Beverly Hills; Sage Publications, 1980), pp. 105–115.

45. *Dothard v. Rawlinson* (433 US 321 [1977]). See E. Matusewitch, "Equal Opportunity for Female Correctional Officers: A Brief Overview," *Corrections Today* 42, no. 4 (November//December 1980): 36–37; and J. Jacobs, "The Sexual Segregation of the Prison's Guard Force: A Few Comments on *Dothard v. Rawlinson*," *University of Toledo Law Review* 10 (1979): 389–418.

46. *Gunther v. Iowa State Men's Reformatory* (462 F. Supp. 952 [N.D. Iowa 1979]).

47. S. Nicolai, "The Upward Mobility of Women in Corrections," in *Prison Guard/Correctional Officer*, p. 54; also, J. Potter, "Should Women Guards Work in Prisons for Men?" *Corrections Magazine* 6, no. 5 (1980): 30–38.

48. L. Zimmer, "Female Guards in Men's Prisons: A Preliminary Report on the Situation in New York and Rhode Island," Unpublished manuscript, 1981; and L. Zupan, "Gender Related Differences in C.O.'s Perceptions and Attitudes."

49. C. Peterson, "Doing Time with the Boys: An Analysis of Women Correctional Officers in All Male Facilities," in *The Criminal Justice System and Women*, ed. B. Price and N. Sokoloff (New York: Clark Boardman and Company, 1982), pp. 437–63.

50. P. Kissel and J. Seidel, *The Management and Impact of Female Corrections Officers at Jail Facilities Housing Male Inmates* (Boulder, CO: National Institute of Corrections, 1980).

51. Zimmer, "Female Guards in Men's Prisons."

52. J. Chapman, *Women Employed in Corrections* (Washington, D.C.: National Institute of Justice, 1983).

53. Zimmer, "Female Guards in Men's Prisons"; also see L. Zupan, "Gender Related Differences in C.O.'s Perceptions and Attitudes."

54. G. Alpert, "The Needs of the Judiciary and Misapplication of Social Research," *Criminology* 22, no. 3 (1984): 441–447.

55. C. Epstein, "Sex Role Stereotyping, Occupations and Social Exchange," *Women's Studies* 3 (1976): 185–94; J. Lipman-Blumen and A. Tickamyer, "Sex Roles in Transition: A Ten Year Perspective," *Annual Review of Sociology* I (1975): 297–337.

56. G. Marret, "Centralization in Female Organizations: Reassessing the Evidence," *Social Problems* 19 (Winter 1972): 221–26.

57. B. Grandjean and H. Bernal, "Sex and Centralization in a Semi-Profession," *Sociology of Work and Occupations*', 6, no. 1 (1979), 84–103.

58. J. Miller, "Women and Work: The Psychological Effects of Occupational Conditions," *American Journal of Sociology* 85 (1979): 77; also, G. Peterson, S. Kiesler and P. Goldberg, "Evaluation of the Performance of Women as a Function of Their Sex, Achievement and Personal History," *Journal of Personality and Social Psychology* 19 (1971): 110–14.

59. W. Wolf and N. Fligstein, "Sex and Authority in the Workplace: The Causes of Sexual Inequality," *American Sociological Review* 44 (1979): 235–52.

60. D. Haccoun et al., "Sex Differences in the Appropriateness of Supervisory Styles: A Management View," *Journal of Applied Psychology* 63 (1978): 124–27.

61. R. Mai-Dalton, "Effect of Employee Gender and Behavior Style on the Evaluation of Men and Women Banking Executives," *Journal of Applied Psychology* 64 (1979): 221–26.

62. M. Zelditch, "Role Differentation in the Nuclear Family," in *Family, Socialization and Interaction*, ed. T. Parsons and R. Bales (New York: Free Press, 1955), 307–353.

63. J. Lipman-Blumen and A. Tickamyer, "Sex Roles in Transition: A Ten Year Perspective," 297–337.

64. M. Bayes and P. Newton, "Women in Authority: A Sociopsychological Analysis," *Journal of Applied Behavioral Science* 14, no. 1 (1978): 7–28.

65. J. Hill, "Therapist Goals, Patient Aims and Patient Satisfaction in Psychotherapy," *Journal of Clinical Psychology* 25 (1969): 445.

2

Males and Females in Prison

INSTITUTIONAL DIFFERENCES

Historical accounts show that the first separate facilities for women which appeared in this country in the early 1800s were quite different from the established prisons at that time for men. While the first institutions for women were often described as "homes," the contemporaneous prisons for men were more often likened to "factories."[1] As women's prisons were built, architectural differences were apparent. For instance, cottages were built in place of the large tiers found in male facilities, and small kitchens were installed in the women's cottages instead of central dining facilities. In many ways, the female facilities were patterned after juvenile reformatories, which were also built to house populations considered less dangerous and more reformable than adult male populations.

Current literature reveals that this architectural heritage, in addition to what it symbolized, lingers on. Recent comments exemplify first impressions of two different women's prisons today. The first is from a prison researcher: "Most inmates live singly in rooms with curtained windows, bedspreads, rugs, and wooden doors. These buildings with soft chairs, couches, and a fireplace, picture windows, and open-out windows for each inmate's room, give the appearance of a convalescent hospital."[2] The second describes the initial impressions of a female inmate: "When I came through the gate, I said to myself: 'This is a

prison?', all the trees and flowers—I couldn't believe it. It looked
like a college with the buildings, the trees, and all the flowers."[3]

Architectural plans for women's prisons still include specifi-
cations linked to the fact that the residents will be women. For
instance, one design called for a less stringent emphasis on security; a "beauticians and hairdressing parlour, where prisoners
could learn the art of hairdressing and make-up," and a "community building to learn whatever domestic or vocational skill
they might be interested in, from shorthand and typing to
cooking."[4]

One other very noticeable architectural difference between
prisons for men and women is their size. Because there are so
few women incarcerated in proportion to the number of men
(roughly 4 percent), the institutions for women are extremely
small, never housing over 500 inmates, while prisons for men
may be two, three, or four times as large. The small size of most
female institutions affects inmates in a number of ways, as described in part by the following:

> The small number of female prisoners as compared with males leads
> to differences in remoteness, heterogeneity and institutional services.
> Some states have so few incarcerated female offenders that they house
> them in adjacent jurisdictions. Even in the larger states, there are not
> enough women offenders to permit classifying them into different in-
> stitutions by custody grading the way it is done with men. It is difficult
> for states to provide adequate religious, medical and other specialized
> institutionalized services to small groups of female prisoners.[5]

The small size also influences the interactions which take place
within the facility. Women's institutions have been described as
lacking the depersonalized atmosphere of male prisons.[6] Small
size has been mentioned as a positive element in juvenile institutions because it "affects the ease in which staff can control and
supervise relationships among youth" and allows staff to "control
peer intimidation."[7] However, it has also been pointed to as a
source of irritation by women inmates who resent the intense
supervision made possible by smaller numbers. It is obvious that
the size factor prevents disaggregation of female inmates, forc-
ing the same staff to deal with a variety of offenders from mur-

derers to check forgers. A single institution for women also eliminates the option of transferring troublemakers or other inmates for protective or control purposes.

Correlated with size is the problem of resources. Studies have shown that prisons for women suffer from inadequate facilities, insufficient staff, limited programs and inappropriate inmate training programs, consisting largely of sewing and cooking lessons.[8] Of course it is also true that male prisons suffer similar problems; however, women's prisons have been criticized for not addressing the current needs of women by failing to provide programs to help them learn job skills instead of domestic skills and for not providing even the minimal vocational programming which is available in prisons for men.

INDIVIDUAL DIFFERENCES

Most comparative descriptions of male and female inmates cover constellations of behavior and personality traits. For instance, the following describes women inmates in 1862:

It is a harder task to manage female prisoners than male. . . . They are more impulsive, more individual, more unreasonable and excitable than men; will not act in concert, and cannot be disciplined in masses. Each wants personal and peculiar treatment, so that the duties fall much more heavily on the matrons than on the warders; matrons having thus to deal with units, not aggregates, and having to adapt themselves to each individual case, instead of simply obeying certain fixed laws and making others obey them, as in the prison for males.[9]

In this one quote a variety of personality traits have been described, including greater emotionality marked by impulsiveness and excitability, unreasonableness, and the need for individual attention. Usually these composite descriptions are ambiguous in terms of whether differences are regarded as biologically caused or as produced by different socialization patterns.

Any given personality trait may be caused by one or a combination of factors. The Eysencks, in their study, found that female prisoners had higher psychoticism scores than male prisoners. A high score on this scale would describe a person with the following characteristics: (1) solitary, not caring for people; (2) cruel, inhumane; (3) troublesome, not fitting in; (4) lack of feeling, insensitive; (5) sensation-seeking; (6) hostile to others, aggressive; (7) liking for odd, unusual things; (8) disregard for danger; and (9) tending to make fools of other people.[10] The Eysencks explained this unexpected finding by hypothesizing that since prison is an infrequently used sentence for women, those who end up there may be more likely than male inmates to have severe psychological problems.

Another study reported MMPI (Minnesota Multiphasic Personality Inventory) test scores of male and female prisoners matched for age, race, IQ, and education. The author found that male inmates' scores indicated they were more prone to voice physical complaints, were more pessimistic in their outlook on life, and more inclined toward irritability and emotional immaturity.[11] Women, on the other hand, were significantly more inclined toward withdrawal from social intercourse and displayed more paranoid reactions.[12] The author found that the higher female scores on the measurement of paranoid reactions were primarily due to the subscale that measured feelings of sensitivity, subjectivity, and being different and not easily understood by others.[13] A study by Warman and Hannum measured MMPI pattern changes in female prisoners and found that women inmates, in contrast to male inmates, became more alike over time in depression, hysteria, and masculinity.[14]

One other study also showed significant differences between male and female prisoners as measured by the MMPI. This author found that women prisoners scored higher on the "Ap" ("prison adjustment") scale, which predicts acting out, hostile responses to custodial stress and confinement, and deliberate violation of prison rules and regulations. Males scored higher on the "Ec" ("prison escape") scale, which suggests a propensity to escape as an adaptation to stress. Men also scored higher on the "A" scale, which is interpreted to mean that a male inmate is overly submissive to authority and lacks confidence in decision making; they also scored higher on a scale measuring psychopathic deviance (Pd). Males scored higher on defects of inhibition control, hypochondria, depression, hysteria, paranoia, obsessive-compulsiveness, schizophrenia, and introversion. Females scored higher on conforming attitudes towards prison rules and defensiveness against personality weakness.[15] The most interesting finding in this study was that women showed more conforming attitudes towards prison authority, but at the same time scored higher on hostile acting out.

There has been an assumption in some literature that women prisoners suffer from low self-esteem compared to women in general. Studies have found no significant differences or have measured increased self-esteem during incarceration, neither of which lends support to the above assumption.[16]

Differences in the Needs of Male and Female Inmates

A number of studies have been done on differences in the management of prisons for men and prisons for women, concentrating on the different needs and problems that women have. One such difference is that a great number of incarcerated women are mothers. The economic, personal, and emotional problems for the inmate mother, i.e., being separated from her child, feeling isolated from the child's growth, being unable to act upon financial or school problems, and experiencing anxiety about reuniting with the child, can also reverberate into problems for the prison.[17]

It is clear from other studies that many prison administrators recognize and accept the responsibilities of providing programs and support to maintain the mother-child relationship. For instance, in one survey, 77 percent of administrators who responded agreed with the statement: "Prisons have the responsibility of establishing programs to help maintain relationships between children and their incarcerated mothers."[18]

Another example of a difference in needs between male and female inmates is the greater demand for medical services and counseling services in prisons for women.[19] Women are more frequent users of medical services outside prison, and this pattern of use persists and may become even more extreme inside prison walls. One explanation for women's more frequent visits to doctors is a difference in the socialization of men and women.

While men are expected to "suffer silently," women enjoy greater freedom to voice physical complaints and are also less apt to suppress them. It may also be that women are more prone to suffer from physical maladies that require medical care, such as gynecological problems. In prison, these general forces may be at work along with exacerbating factors peculiar to the prison environment, such as loneliness, a need for attention, boredom, a pattern of drug use and lack of medical care before incarceration, all of which combine to produce disproportionate requests for medical care by women inmates.

Behavioral Differences

Several types of behavioral differences between incarcerated men and women have been explored. Findings indicate that there are different patterns of homosexual activity in male and female prisons. While male homosexual activity has been characterized as aggressive, predatory, and often violent; female homosexuality has been described as endemic but consensual. There is a type of relationship among female inmates described in the literature as "make-believe" or "pseudo" families. It seems that these family relationships accompany homosexual dyads or exist separately from dyads in female institutions.[20]

In an early study, Selling concluded that the inmate "families" were natural substitutes for families outside the prison, and that prison family groupings were nonpathological examples of lesbianism. Selling distinguished four stages of inmate activity: (a) lesbianism; (b) pseudohomosexuality; (c) mother-daughter relationships; and (d) friendships. Nothing similar to these family systems has been found in prisons for men.[21] The gang structure, of course, is the best known male social organization, and there are many differences between its hierarchical "political" structure and the relational-affectional structure of female "families."

Another version of homosexuality was offered by Hammer, who hypothesized that female inmates were involved in rejecting their own passivity and dependency to pursue a more active, aggressive, and masculine way of life in order to master feelings of helplessness and vulnerability. Hammer further presupposed that those who engage in homosexual contacts do so because of a need for a pre-oedipal mother to whom they could once again become attached. The older woman in the relationship was portrayed as loving an extension of herself, giving the mothering she would like to have received herself. In comparison, male homosexuality has been described as a means to degrade and subordinate a weaker individual in addition to being a means to obtain sexual gratification.[22]

Halleck and Herski attempted to pin down the amount of homosexuality which occurred in one female institution. They found that in an institution for adolescents, 69 percent of fifty-seven recently released girls admitted some amount of involvement, although only 5 percent described actual genital stimulation. This finding is supported by other studies which show relatively small proportions of flagrant homosexual activity in relation to more pseudohomosexual activity, i.e., holding hands, kissing, or writing love letters. The situation in male prisons seems to be that a smaller proportion of homosexual involvement is reported, but that a larger percentage of it is genital rather than social.[23]

According to Giallombardo, different (gender-related) experiences in the free world cause male and female inmates to experience the pains of imprisonment differently. Women disproportionately feel the loss of self-image caused by removal of family roles (wife, mother, daughter), and they create substitute family systems in response. Societal norms also make it more likely for homosexuality to develop among women because women are allowed to express affection in public by kissing and hugging, and because women are assumed to have more emotional attachments. Also, the family system flourishes because women do not trust each other and form relationships to guard against being cheated or hurt by other inmates.[24]

Ward and Kassebaum published their study about the same time as Giallombardo and reached somewhat similar conclusions, although they used different methods (primarily interviews and questionnaires, while Giallombardo used participant observation). Fifty percent of the inmates who completed Ward and Kassebaum's questionnaire admitted they were somewhat involved in the inmate culture of homosexuality. Ward and Kassebaum maintained that homosexuality was an adaptation to the pains of imprisonment, primarily the deprivation of emotional attachments and isolation in a hostile environment.[25]

One may use the reasoning implicit in these deprivation arguments to explain male homosexuality also; i.e., males are deprived of a means of asserting their masculinity in the absence of women and must find other targets to "prove" they are men. In other words, the heterosexual relationship provides women with emotional attachments and affection while it provides men with an affirmation of masculinity. In prison, deprived of the opposite sex, men and women find means to fulfill these needs through homosexual relationships.

Somewhat related studies have tested the hypothesis that women in prison are more masculine than women on the outside. One of these studies attempted to associate masculinity with homosexual behavior in prison.[26] The "stud" role of the female inmate subculture parodies masculine characteristics in dress and mannerisms, but researchers have been interested in (a) whether all incarcerated women tend to possess masculine values or personality traits; and (b) whether those who "act" like males in prison carry these traits outside the prison setting or are merely acting a role.

Several theorists have subscribed to the idea that criminal women are more "masculine" than law-abiding women.[27] A modern version of this theory is that women's liberation is positively associated with a rise of violent crime among women.[28] One study charted masculine and feminine activities of incarcerated women in a prison classroom. The masculinity/femininity scores assigned to each woman were used as variables in a study of the relationship between masculinity/femininity, leadership, and homosexual activity. The author found no relationship between masculinity and leadership, but did find that homosexually active women scored higher on masculinity. Unfortunately, there were many problems with this study, such as scores based on stereotyped behavior that was subjectively labeled masculine or feminine, and inmates labeled homosexual based on hearsay testimony from five informants.[29]

Another group of researchers have hypothesized that black women are overrepresented in crime because they are socialized to perform "male" societal functions such as supporting families.

Additionally, both black females and black males are raised to be "assertive, non-conforming, independent, nurturing, expressive emotionally, and focused in personal relationships."[30] Since these traits are differentially ascribed by sex in the white culture, the presence of some of them among black women leads to a perception that black women are more "masculine" than white women. Since black women comprise roughly 50 percent of most prison populations, this inference may affect the perception of female prisoners as masculine.[31]

In addition to being seen as more masculine, women in prison are commonly characterized as having the least desirable of what are thought to be female traits (untrustworthiness, flightiness, jealousy, deceitfulness, and so on).[32] Smart discusses the perception that females share some qualities of the mentally ill, such as irrationality, compulsiveness, and neuroticism; she notes the assumption that these qualities exist to an even greater degree among incarcerated women.[33]

Social Organization

With respect to patterns of social organization, Maccoby and Jacklin report on early tendencies of girls to form "chumships" and to cultivate small groups of friends.[34] A similar tendency among adult women was found in a study of the differences between male and female inmate social organization under forced confinement in a drug treatment hospital.[35]

Scharf and Hickey found differences in the social patterns of male and female inmates in two self-governing "communities" established as part of an experiment in a Connecticut prison. They described the men's unit as adversarial, with a greater degree of social distance between male inmates and staff members and between male inmates themselves. There developed much closer attachments between group members and staff in the women's groups. During meetings in the female unit there were many exchanges regarding feelings and attitudes towards both staff and other inmates; while in meetings which took place in the men's unit, the topics discussed dealt almost exclusively with cottage conflicts, rules, and tension. Female inmates seemed oriented toward a greater sense of community than the men,

but in the male unit there existed a political consciousness that
was absent among the women. The authors called the two sex-
related styles "communitarian" and "political," but cautioned
that these different styles could have arisen through factors other
than sex differences.[36]

Another study predicted that because the custodial control of
a women's prison was less restrictive than that found in a prison
for men, one might find a weaker inmate subculture. It was
predicted that the women's response might be one of "individ-
uality, pulling one's own time, or, in short, a lack of concern
for fellow inmates in either their problems or their pleas-
ures."[37] Kruttschnitt's study supports this prediction in its
finding that although women expressed opposition to staff (74
percent), a majority did not endorse other tenets of an "inmate
code" (60 percent). The author concluded that women's prisons may contain a "subculture of inmates" rather than an "inmate subculture."[38]

Two other studies examined women's adherence to an inmate
subculture. Jensen found that 50 percent of his sample of women
inmates subscribed to an inmate code, while Sieverdes and Bartollas found that 61 percent of their sample "strongly adhered"
to an inmate subculture.[39] It is clear that more work needs to be
done to resolve these discrepancies. Intervening variables such
as age, race, and type of offense or facility may be the reason
why Kruttschnitt's findings are different from Jensen's and from
Sieverdes and Bartollas's.

Also, these findings must be interpreted with the realization
that many recent studies of male inmates fail to find the strong
adherence to the "inmate subculture" described by early prison
researchers. It may be the case that the descriptions of a strong
subculture developed in the 1950s do not exist in either prisons
for men or women today.[40]

Acting Out Behavior

The literature on gender differences tells us that males are
more aggressive than females. The evidence that the difference
in the aggressivity between males and females is biologically
caused includes the following elements: (1) males are more ag-

gressive than females in all human societies; (2) sex differences
are found early in life before socialization; (3) similar sex differences are found in subhuman primates; and (4) aggression
can be manipulated by increasing or decreasing sex hormones.[41]

Arrest statistics certainly indicate that women do not engage
in assaultive behavior (or at least are not arrested for such behavior) as frequently as men.[42] However, in correctional institutions, what evidence we have seems to support the view that
females engage in all sorts of acting out behavior, including
assaultiveness, more frequently than incarcerated males.

One unpublished report compiled by the research department
of the Department of Correctional Services in New York indicates that Bedford Hills (a prison for women in New York) had
the highest rate of assaults in the New York Correctional System.
One assault per 24.8 inmates was recorded for Bedford Hills,
while the next highest rate (one assault for every 27.7 inmates)
occurred in Great Meadow Correctional Facility. Interestingly,
the demographic description of an assaulter was the same for
men and women. Both male and female assaulters tend to be
young, black, and incarcerated for a violent crime. The major
difference between the assaults by females and males was in the
type of method of assault. A larger number of the women's
assaults were not put into categories such as punching/shoving
or stabbing, but were recorded in a miscellaneous category identified as "other."[43]

Although there are problems with studies which attempt to
compare rates between different types of facilities which typically
do not have similar reporting procedures, the findings of the
New York study do not stand alone. Lindquist similarly reports
that both male and female assaulters were likely to be young and
black. He also found that "the average female disciplinary offender committed significantly more offenses (4.38) than their
male counterparts (2.61); however, . . . the latter committed significantly more serious offenses."[44]

There is a great deal of evidence in the literature to suggest
that women engage in various types of acting out behavior more
frequently than men. In one study, matched samples of thirty
male and thirty female hospitalized mental patients were selected
and paired for age, intelligence, classification, and length of in-

stitutionalization. An analysis was made of aggressive behavior using the following categories: aggression to person, aggression to property, aggression to self, causing a noisy disturbance, and aggression related to psychiatric symptoms. The authors found that the women had higher rates for all these categories of behavior.[45]

One explanation offered for these findings was that psychopathic women had a lower threshold for frustration than psychopathic men. Another theory, which may be called the "overflow theory," holds that women more rapidly reach the stage where the emotional components of aggression, anger, or tension are channeled into physical activity of some kind in order to discharge the internal stress. A related explanation is that feelings of anxiety and subjective stress cause aggression to erupt spontaneously in women.

It seems to be a widely held belief that women use behavior as a means of self-expression rather than to achieve rational goals. Studies have indicated, for instance, that boys commit delinquent acts to gain status while girls often commit delinquent acts as a direct expression of hostility or in response to other needs.[46] The outbursts of female prisoners are similarly characterized as "irrational, uncontrolled, diffuse and not goal oriented."[47]

Two studies have been done which look at those prisoners who injure themselves in some way. Cookson found that women who hurt themselves in prison were more impulsive, particularly in an "intropunitive" direction. The self-destructiveness of the inmates was attributed to a sense of depersonalization connected with depression or tension, hostility or aggression towards the institution or their family. Other possible reasons cited for self-destructiveness were attention-seeking and chronic boredom.[48] These are not necessarily different from the motivations of male inmates who injure themselves.

Fox, as part of a larger study of prisoner breakdowns, found female self-destructiveness to be frustration-centered. The most prominent theme he recorded was a need for support from significant others; this was different from the most prevalent themes for males, which included a pervasive sense of failure or unworthiness.[49]

It is hard to reconcile the evidence that females are more aggressive, both to themselves and to others, with our common stereotype of females as passive and nonaggressive. To date, no attempts have been made to reconcile these findings and assumptions.

Values and Attitudes

One other subject dealt with in prison literature is that of differences in the values and attitudes of incarcerated men and women. One study has suggested that women inmates are more likely to be conformist and males are more likely to be anti-authoritarian (rebellious); this hypothesis was tested and confirmed using an incomplete sentences test administered to sixty-three inmates.[50]

Other studies, however, have found that female prisoners exhibit significantly more negative attitudes towards the criminal justice system. Kay studied Ohio reformatory women using the Mylonas Attitudes to Law and Legal Institutions scale, the Crissman Moral Values scale, and the Gough socialization scale. These findings indicated that females held more negative views of the system than male inmates, as measured by all of the above scales. The author of the study identified a "feline syndrome" which involved the tendency of women to take "things to heart" more readily than men, and to have longer memories for inequities.[51]

In speculating about why such differences in attitudes occur, one might again consider the fact that women who are studied in prison are generally a smaller percentage of the female criminal population than men in prison (since fewer women are incarcerated),[52] or that women actually do receive worse treatment from the system justifying resentment (e.g., lawyers expecting sexual favors).[53] Alternatively, it might be that such attitudes exist because of gender-related personality traits such as a propensity for avoidance of blame. This does not have much support in the literature since a study of the tendency to blame others found that both sexes placed the blame for their actions on others, only that males found blame with peers while females found blame with their families.[54]

Studies classifying subjects using Kohlberg's moral stages find that women score proportionately higher in the stage of "good boy or girl," a level just below the stage of law and order morality and just above a stage concerned with punishment, both of which contain clusterings of males.[55] One might deduce from this that males are concerned with power (law and order morality) and recognize and play by "rules of the game" (accepting punishment when caught), while females take punishment more personally since it is more damaging to their self-concept as "good." A study which gives peripheral support to the assumption that males place a greater emphasis on control was done using male and females diagnosed as sociopaths. The variable most salient for risk taking among men was avoidance of censure, but among women, maximization of gain was more important than any other factor, indicating that women were less aware of punishment contingencies.[56]

Summary

The above studies have all described and/or compared males and females in prison. Adjectives used to describe females include: impulsive, individualistic, unreasonable, excitable, depressed, hysterical, masculine, untrustworthy, flighty, jealous, deceitful, irrational, compulsive, neurotic, aggressive, manipulative, attention-seeking, and conformist. Female inmates have also been described as needing individual attention; being withdrawn from social intercourse; displaying paranoid reactions; showing sensitivity; being overly subjective; possessing feelings of being "different" and not easily understood; having feelings of isolation; lacking gratification in social relationships; acting out with hostility; violating prison rules; having low self-esteem; having problems with children; having greater needs for medical care and counseling services; being more likely to get involved with the homosexual subculture; having greater attachments to each other; forming smaller groups; having associations that tend to be emotionally based; engaging in outbursts that tend to be irrational, uncontrolled, diffuse, and not goal-directed; taking things "to heart"; needing support from significant others; and having significantly more negative attitudes towards the criminal justice system.

Males, on the other hand, were described as extroverted, aggressive, having a penchant for authority conflicts, being escape prone, overly submissive to authority, inclined toward irritability and emotional immaturity, psychopathically deviant, having trouble with inhibition control, and being hypochondriac. In addition, males would be expected to form larger groups, have associations that tend to be political and issue-oriented, and to be anti-authoritarian in orientation.

CORRECTIONAL OFFICER PERCEPTIONS

We must stress that what is reported in this section are the officers' views regarding what they have seen and experienced. This data (collected by interview) is a collection of officers' perceptions. While these officers have a great deal of experience in the prison system with both male and female inmates, we do not assume they are completely unbiased recorders of inmate behavior. Bias conditions what any of us choose to remember, what importance is placed on a particular event, what is determined to be serious or not, and so on. If our interviews suggest, as they do, that complaints from women are deemed trivial, this may, in fact, be a valid assessment, but it may also be true that the officers are predisposed to regard any complaints of female inmates as trivial. Likewise, what officers regard as an irrational emotional outburst from a women might be deemed rational if similar behavior is performed by a man. Despite these cautions, the interviews we conducted suggest that officers can be very sympathetic and sensitive observers of human nature. Many, if not most, interviewees showed great insight into inmates' motivations and the meaning behind the behavior of both men and women in prison.

The results from an adjective checklist are presented in Table 1. From this table we can see how the sample of officers perceive male and female inmates. First of all, it is interesting to note those adjectives which are applied frequently to both male and female inmates. According to officers, both male and female inmates are defensive (54.5%), distrustful (50%), and manipulative (65%).[57]

We can also determine which adjectives are applied frequently

Table 1
Traits Attributed by Officers to Male and Female Inmates[1]

Adjective	Number of officers who checked adjective for males		Number of officers who checked adjective for females		Difference
irresponsible	40%	(17)	40%	(17)	0
honest	10%	(4)	10%	(4)	0
lazy	29%	(12)	29%	(12)	0
cynical	24%	(10)	24%	(10)	0
aggressive	55%	(23)	55%	(23)	0
distrustful	50%	(21)	50%	(21)	0
dependent	19%	(8)	21%	(9)	2
evasive	40%	(17)	38%	(16)	2
kind	12%	(5)	14%	(6)	2
cruel	17%	(7)	19%	(8)	2
aloof	19%	(8)	14%	(6)	5
rebellious	43%	(18)	36%	(15)	7
suspicious	52%	(22)	45%	(19)	7
arrogant	29%	(12)	36%	(15)	7
stubborn	33%	(14)	40%	(17)	7
impulsive	40%	(17)	48%	(20)	8
defensive	60%	(25)	50%	(21)	10
anxious	33%	(14)	43%	(18)	10
self-punishing	10%	(4)	21%	(9)	11
manipulative	60%	(25)	71%	(30)	11
confident	21%	(9)	10%	(4)	11
bossy	12%	(5)	24%	(10)	12
considerate	36%	(15)	21%	(9)	15
noisy	48%	(20)	64%	(27)	16
self-centered	26%	(11)	43%	(18)	17
hostile	26%	(11)	43%	(18)	17
deceitful	29%	(12)	48%	(20)	19
immature	43%	(18)	62%	(26)	19
irritable	14%	(6)	36%	(15)	22
vindictive	29%	(12)	55%	(23)	24
touchy	31%	(13)	55%	(23)	24
capable	43%	(18)	17%	(7)	26
assertive	45%	(19)	19%	(8)	26
excitable	38%	(16)	64%	(27)	26
headstrong	48%	(20)	21%	(9)	27
tough	38%	(16)	10%	(4)	28
argumentative	40%	(17)	69%	(29)	29
active	64%	(27)	31%	(13)	33
sensitive	12%	(5)	45%	(19)	33
changeable	33%	(14)	67%	(28)	34
complaining	43%	(18)	81%	(34)	38
boastful	57%	(24)	19%	(8)	38
highstrung	12%	(5)	50%	(21)	38
demanding	31%	(13)	69%	(29)	38
quarrelsome	17%	(7)	64%	(27)	47
moody	24%	(10)	74%	(31)	50
emotional	29%	(12)	83%	(35)	54
temperamental	19%	(8)	76%	(32)	57

[1](N=42); a test was done for dependent samples, matched pairs using the t distribution and it was found that the adjectives as a group were differentially applied to men and women (significant at the .001 level).

to either sex. As expected, women were characterized as emotional (83%), temperamental (76%), moody (74%), manipulative (71%), quarrelsome (64%), demanding (69%), changeable (67%), complaining (81%), argumentative (69%), excitable (64%), immature (62%), and noisy (64%). Men, on the other hand, were depicted as active (64%), defensive (60%), boastful (57%), aggressive (55%), and manipulative (60%).[58]

There was much less consensus among the officers in applying adjectives to males, which raises the possibility that officers possess a stereotype of females. It is not unusual to obtain a high rate of agreement among those who possess a common stereotype of a group; likewise, one is less likely to get consensus on a description of any group when a stereotype is not operating, since people interact and perceive each other differently. In our sample, only three adjectives for males were agreed upon by more than 60 percent of the officers, whereas 60 percent or more officers agreed on twelve adjectives for females.

Another concern of the table is the degree of the differential between adjectives attributed to the sexes. We are interested in those adjectives which were applied more frequently to males than females or vice versa. We find, for instance, that six of the adjectives (irresponsible, honest, lazy, cynical, aggressive, and distrustful) were used by a similar number of officers to describe males and females. Thus, these adjectives were not applied differentially. The adjective "temperamental," however, was applied to females by 59.8 percent of the officers, but no officers perceived only men as temperamental. A statistical test (Table 2) confirms that there are adjectives in the table that are differentially applied to male and female inmates.

In our interview we encouraged the officers to supplement and elaborate upon their "mini-portraits" of male and female inmates. Interview queries about perceived differences between men and women demanded greater thought, and because the question was open-ended, there was less consensus in these officer responses. However, a content analysis of the responses resulted in identifying three major themes.

The first theme was labeled "defiance" and involved descriptions of women opposing or "standing up" to the officers in various ways. Responses falling into this category included the

Table 2
Test of Significance for Differentially Applied Adjectives[1]

Officers Applied This Adjective to:

Adjective	Both	Males	Females	Neither	Sign.
irresponsible	11	6	7	18	
honest	2	1	3	36	
lazy	7	7	6	22	
cynical	7	3	4	28	
aggressive	16	7	8	11	
distrustful	15	6	6	15	
dependent	3	6	6	27	
evasive	11	4	5	22	
kind	3	2	3	34	
cruel	2	5	6	29	
aloof	2	6	4	30	
rebellious	9	9	7	17	
suspicious	14	8	5	15	
arrogant	7	6	7	22	
stubborn	11	3	6	22	
impulsive	12	4	8	18	
defensive	17	8	4	13	
anxious	10	4	8	20	
assertive	3	10	4	25	
self-punishing	1	3	8	30	
bossy	3	2	7	30	
munipulative	19	5	10	8	
confident	3	6	1	32	
considerate	1	13	9	19	
self-centered	10	1	9	22	
hostile	8	3	11	20	
noisy	16	4	11	11	
deceitful	10	3	11	18	
immature	16	3	12	1	*
irritable	4	2	11	25	*
vindictive	11	1	12	18	**
headstrong	6	14	3	19	*
capable	5	13	2	22	**
excitable	14	2	12	14	*
argumentative	14	5	15	9	
tough	3	13	1	25	**
changeable	13	1	14	13	**
active	13	14	1	14	**
sensitive	4	2	15	21	**
touchy	9	5	15	13	*
complaining	13	3	21	5	**
boastful	6	18	2	16	**
highstrung	3	3	17	19	**
demanding	11	2	18	11	**
quarrelsome	7	0	21	14	**
moody	10	0	11	21	**
emotional	4	3	31	4	
temperamental	8	0	25	9	

[1](N=42); Fisher's Exact Test was used to determine significance;
*=.05 level; **.01 level of significance.

following: "argumentative," "less likely to follow rules," "demanding," "harder to handle," "question rules," "more troublesome," "more complaining," "confront you verbally," "don't accept no," "more critical," "less respectful," and "harder to reason with." Fifty-three percent of the officers had some element of this theme in their responses.

The second theme described an "open display of emotion" on the part of women. This theme identified a tendency among women to verbalize and act out emotion rather than to keep it hidden. Officers' responses in this area included "more feeling," "louder," "holler and scream more," "greater tendency to cry," "noisy," "spur of the moment outbreaks," "fight spontaneously," "ready to explode," "cry-babies," "explosive," "lose temper easily," "fight easily," and, "give vent to their emotions." This theme was found in 51 percent of the responses.

The third theme identified was labeled "gratification seeking" and involved characterizations which described the women as needing and wanting more from their environment than men; both material and personal commodities, such as attention, friendship, or sympathy. An added component of this theme was the element of wanting things immediately with little or no patience or willingness to wait. Representative responses include "looking for sympathy," "susceptible to peer pressure," "talk about problems," "emotionally demanding," "being friendly," "less independent," "more dependent," "more childish," "less patient," "demands are critical," "greater need for friends," and "inquisitive." Twenty-eight percent of the officers' responses contained some aspect of this theme.

After the initial probe regarding differences between men and women, officers were asked to agree or disagree with a series of questions phrased as "were women inmates more—than male inmates?" Table 3 presents the officers' responses to these probes.

Officers did not feel women were more unpredictable, childish, or assertive than men. They also did not feel women were more likely to mutilate themselves, have a greater need for counselors, or use more prescription drugs. Only 18 percent of the officers believed that women were more likely to possess a guilty conscience. Most of the officers believed either that no inmate experienced guilt or that one could never discover whether they did or not.

Table 3
Officers' Responses to Interview Probes[1]

Question	Number of Officers Who Responded		
	Yes	No	Sign.
Are women more emotional?	89% (40)	11% (5)	**
Are women more demanding?	84% (38)	16% (7)	**
Are women more complaining	71% (32)	29% (13)	**
Are women more open?	62% (28)	38% (17)	*
Are women easier to get to know?	36% (16)	64% (29)	*
Are women more manipulative?	62% (28)	38% (17)	*
Are women more unpredictable?	64% (29)	22% (10)[2]	
Are women more childish?	44% (21)	53% (24)	
Are women more dishonest?	22% (10)	78% (35)	**
Are women more irresponsible?	36% (16)	64% (29)	**
Are women more assertive	60% (27)	40% (18)	
Are women more assaultive towards inmates?	49% (22)	51% (23)	
Are women more assaultive towards officers?	33% (15)	67% (30)	**
Do women self-multilate more?	58% (26)	42% (19)	
Do women have less self-esteem?	24% (11)	76% (34)	**
Do women more often have a guilty conscience?	18% (8)	82% (37)	**
Do women have a greater need for counselors?	49% (22)	51% (23)	
Do women have a greater need for medical doctors?	80% (36)	20% (9)	**
Do women "act out" more often?	85% (38)	16% (7)	**
Do women follow orders less often?	67% (30)	33% (15)	*
Does homosexuality among women cause more problems?	60% (27)	40% (18)	
Are women in prison more masculine than women outside?	27% (12)	53% (24)[3]	**
Do women organize less than men?	62% (28)	38% (17)	*
Do women have fewer leaders?	64% (29)	36% (16)	*
Do women have more contraband?	22% (10)	78% (35)	**
Do women use more prescribed drugs?	53% (24)	47% (21)	
Do women have different problems?	78% (35)	22% (10)	**

---

[1](N=45); a difference of proportions test was used comparing the "yes" responses to 50% as a null hypotesis. (*=significant at .05 level) (**=significant at .01 level).

[2]Total is not 100% because 13% (6) of the officers answered "both".

[3]Total is not 100% because 53% (24) of the officers answered "some".

Most of those people carry that guilt and you or I or probably even some of the best psychiatrists will never know. They have to do their time and they have to live their life and if they were to go around living on a guilt trip, they would all go buggy before their time was even up. It's something that they may feel, but they very seldom show it. It's hidden very well within themselves and most people never reach it, they never find it, because basically they couldn't survive. That guilt, if they have any, if that guilt takes over, it would totally destroy them before they finish their time. So it's something they just put aside. (143-female)

Most of the officers interviewed felt that there were no differences in the self-esteem of men and women (76 percent). Interestingly, those 24 percent who felt women had lower self-esteem almost always mentioned societal pressures that may have affected how the women felt about themselves.

I think the self-esteem relates to, you know, the historical role of women in this society. I don't think we can separate that. I think it has a lot to do with their life experiences complicated by the fact that they've had children oft' times unable to provide for them. (P11-female)

Women tended not to feel successful with anything. They didn't feel successful as lovers, they didn't feel successful as mothers ... whereas men felt a lot more success relatively speaking, I found, than the women did. Men could say, "I was a good carpenter" or "I did this well" or "I screwed more women than anybody else on the block." (P5-male)

Officers also did not feel women were more assaultive than men, but there were complexities involved in these responses that bear further study. It seems that many traits, while not differentially applied, are perceived by the officers as manifested differently among male and female inmates. That is, while neither men or women were described as honest, officers perceived that women's dishonesty was enacted in different ways. For instance, when confronted with wrongdoing, women were perceived as more likely to try to explain their way out of their transgressions rather than admit culpability or remain silent.

A lot of times I'll have the adjustment committee where they get a discipline report, and I'll find for the most part, the males are less apt to make excuses for their behavior, less apt to make up a lot of stories to cover what supposedly happened. And the females—it isn't that they fantasize, it's just that they will give you a long dissertation on an "acceptable variation of the charge," "Well, I did it, but....". (I2-female)

They will come out and say they stole something but have a story all the time to explain. (I16-male)

The other element of women being perceived as more dishonest relates to perceived capacity for dissimulation. Officers claimed to be less able to tell when a woman is lying or "telling a story."

In observing, you can almost sense a man being dishonest. I find it easier with them than I do with a woman. (I3-female)

Thus, even though officers did not find there were any differences in the tendency of men or women to be honest or dishonest, the way dishonesty was manifested between the sexes was perceived to be different.

As we shall see in the next chapter, officers describe these various behavior pattern differences of male and female inmates as contributing to the difficulty of their job.

NOTES

1. C. Anderson, "The Female Criminal Offender," *American Journal of Corrections* 29 (1967): 7–9; M. Falconer, "Reformatory Treatment of Women," *Proceedings of the National Conference of Charities and Corrections* (New York: National Conference of Charities and Corrections, 1919), pp. 253–56; and E. C. Lekkerkerker, *Reformatories for Women in the U.S.* (Gronigen, Netherlands: J. B. Wolters, 1931).

2. D. Ward and G. Kassebaum, *Women's Prison: Sex and Social Structure* (Chicago: Aldine, 1965), p. 7.

3. R. Heffernan, *The Square, the Cool and the Life* (New York: John Wiley and Sons, 1972), p. 47.

4. S. Rotner, "Design for a Women's Prison: An Architect's View," *Howard Journal of Penology and Crime Prevention* 11 (1963): 229.

5. L. Bowker, *Women, Crime and the Criminal Justice System* (Lexington, MA: Lexington Books, 1978), p. 229.

6. M. Wheeler, "The Current Status of Women in Prisons," *Criminal Justice and Behavior* 1, no. 4 (1974): 374–80.

7. C. McEwen, "Subcultures in Community Based Programs," in *Juvenile Correctional Reform in Massachusetts*, ed. L. Ohlin, A. Miller and R. Coates (Washington, D.C.: *National Institute for Juvenile Justice*, LEAA, 1972).

8. P. Baunach and T. Murton, "Women in Prison, An Awakening Minority," *Crime and Corrections* 1 (1973): 4–12.

9. Prison Matron, *Female Life in Prison* (New York: Hurst and Blackett, 1862).

10. S.B.G. Eysenck and H. J. Eysenck, "The Personality of Female Prisoners," *British Journal of Psychiatry* 122 (1973): 693–98.

11. J. Panton, "Personality Differences between Male and Female Prison Inmates Measured by the MMPI," *Criminal Justice and Behavior* 1, no. 4 (1974): 332–39 (Hs and D scales).

12. Panton, "Personality Differences," pp. 332–39 (Pa and Si scales).

13. Panton, "Personality Differences," p. 339.

14. R. E. Warman and T. E. Hannum, "MMPI Pattern Changes in Female Prisoners," *Journal of Research in Crime and Delinquency* 2 (1965): 72–76.

15. J. Joesting, N. Jones and R. Joesting, "Male and Female Prison Inmates' Differences on MMPI Scales and Revised Beta IQ," *Psychological Reports* 37, no. 2 (1975): 471–74.

16. B. Payak, "Understanding the Female Offender," *Federal Probation* 27, no. 4. (December 1963): 7–12; C. Widom, "Female Offenders: Three Assumptions about Self-Esteem, Sex-Role Identity and Feminism,"*Criminal Justice and Behavior* 6, no. 4 (1979): 365–82; and T. E. Hannum, F. H. Borgen and R. M. Anderson, "Self-Concept Changes Associated with Incarceration in Female Prisoners," *Criminal Justice and Behavior* 5 no. 3 (1978): 271–79.

17. K. Haley, "Mothers behind Bars: A Look at the Parental Rights of Incarcerated Women," *New England Journal of Prison Law* 4 no. 1 (1977): 141–55; P. Baunach, "Mothering behind Prison Walls," Paper presented at American Society of Criminology Conference, Philadelphia, Pennsylvania, 1979; B. McGowan and K. Blumenthal, *Why Punish the Children?: A Study of Children of Women Prisoners* (Hackensack, N.J.: National Council on Crime and Delinquency, 1978); and R. Palmer, "The Prison Mother and Her Child," *Capital University Law Review* 1 (1972): 127–44.

18. H. Musk, "Programs for Incarcerated Women and Their Children: Final Report," Paper presented at American Society of Criminology Conference, Washington, D.C., 1981.

19. C. Feinman, "Prisons for Women: The Multi-Purpose Institution," Paper presented at American Society of Criminology Conference,

Philadelphia, Pennsylvania, 1979; and J. Eyman, *Prison for Women: A Practical Guide to Administrative Problems* (Springfield, IL: Charles C. Thomas, 1971).

20. Male homosexuality is described in A. Ibrahim, "Deviant Sexual Behavior in Men's Prisons," *Crime and Delinquency* 20 (1974): 41–45; and A. Scacco, *Rape in Prison* (Springfield, IL: Charles C. Thomas, 1975).

21. L. Selling, "The Pseudo-Family," *American Journal of Sociology* 37 (1931): 247–53.

22. M. Hammer, "Homosexuality in a Women's Reformatory," *Corrective Psychiatry and Journal of Social Therapy* 11, no. 3 (1965): 168–69; and "Hypersexuality in Reformatory Women," *Corrective Psychiatry and Journal of Social Therapy* 15, no. 4 (1969): 20–26.

23. S. Halleck and M. Herski, "Homosexual Behavior in a Correctional Institution for Adolescent Girls," *American Journal of Orthopsychiatry* 32 (1962): 911–17.

24. R. Giallombardo, *Society of Women* (New York: John Wiley, 1966), pp. 92–158.

25. Ward and Kassebaum, *Women's Prison*, 80–95.

26. E. Kates, "Sexual Problems in Women's Institutions," *Journal of Social Therapy* 1 (1955): 187–91.

27. C. Lombroso, *The Female Offender* (New York: Appleton, 1920); W. I. Thomas, *The Unadjusted Girl* (Boston: Little, Brown and Company, 1973); O. Pollak, *The Criminality of Women* (New York: A. S. Barnes and Company, 1950); G. Knopka, *The Adolescent Girl in Conflict* (Englewood Cliffs, NJ: Prentice-Hall, 1966); and J. Cowie, J. Cowie and E. Slater, *Delinquency in Girls* (Cambridge, MA: Humanities Press, 1968).

28. F. Adler, *Sisters in Crime* (New York: McGraw-Hill, 1975).

29. K. Van Wormer, "Sex Role Behavior in a Women's Prison: An Ethological Analysis," Dissertation, University of Georgia, 1976.

30. D. Lewis, "Black Women Offenders and Criminal Justice: Some Theoretical Considerations," in *Comparing Female and Male Offenders*, ed. M. Warren (Beverly Hills, CA: Sage Publications, 1981), p. 99.

31. S. Datesman and F. Scarpetti, "Unequal Protection for Males and Females in the Juvenile Court," in *Women, Crime and Justice*, ed S. K. Datesman and F. R. Scarpetti (New York: Oxford University Press, 1980), pp. 300–319; and D. Lewis, "Black Women Offenders and Criminal Justice," 89–106.

32. C. Widom, "Female Offenders"; and C. Smart, *Women, Crime and Criminology: A Feminist Critique* (London: Routledge and Kegan Paul, 1976).

33. C. Smart, *Women, Crime and Criminology*, pp. 146–76.

34. E. Maccoby and C. N. Jacklin, *The Psychology of Sex Differences* (Stanford, CA: Stanford University Press, 1974), pp. 205–211.

35. C. Tittle, "Inmate Organization: Sex Differentiation and the Influence of Criminal Subcultures," *American Sociological Review* 34 (1969): 492–505.

36. P. Scharf and D. Hickey, "Just Community," unpublished draft, 1980.

37. M. Zingraff, "Inmate Assimilation: A Comparison of Male and Female Delinquents," *Criminal Justice and Behavior* 7, no. 3 (1980): 291.

38. C. Kruttschnitt, "Prison Codes, Inmate Solidarity and Women: A Reexamination," in *Comparing Female and Male Offenders*, pp. 123–43.

39. G. Jensen, "Perspectives on Inmate Culture: A Study of Women in Prison," *Social Forces* 54 (1976): 590–603; and C. Sieverdes and B. Bartollas, "Institutional Adjustment Among Female Delinquents," in *Improving Management in Criminal Justice*, ed. A. Cohn and B. Ward (Beverly Hills, CA: Sage Publications, 1982), pp. 91–105.

40. J. Ramierez, "Prisonization, Staff and Inmates: Is it Really Us against Them?" *Criminal Justice and Behavior* 11, no. 4 (1984): 423–60.

41. Maccoby and Jacklin, *Psychology of Sex Differences*, p. 242.

42. R. Simon, *Women and Crime* (Lexington, MA: D. C. Heath and Company, 1975), pp. 33–36; and L. Bowker, *Women and Crime in America* (New York: Macmillan Publishing Company, 1981), pp. 202–207.

43. D. Selksky, "Assaults on Correctional Employees—April, 1979 to March, 1980," Unpublished report, New York Department of Correctional Services, 1980.

44. C. Lindquist, "Prison Discipline and the Female Offender," *Journal of Offender Counseling*, Services and Rehabilitation 4, no. 4 (1980): 307.

45. D. W. McKerracher, D.R.K. Street and L. S. Segal, "A Comparison of the Behavior Problems Presented by Male and Female Subnormal Offenders," *British Journal of Psychiatry* 112 (1966): 891–99.

46. G. Barker and W. Adams, "Comparison of the Delinquency of Boys and Girls," *Journal of Criminal Law, Criminology and Police Science* 53 (1962): 470–75.

47. A. Novick, "The Make-Believe Family: Informal Group Structure among Institutionalized Delinquent Girls," in *Casework Papers from the National Conference on Social Welfare* (New York: New York Family Service Association of America, 1960), pp. 44–59.

48. H. M. Cookson, "Survey of Self-Injury in a Closed Prison for Women," *British Journal of Criminology* 17, no. 4 (1977): 332–47.

49. J. Fox, "Women in Crisis," in *Men in Crisis* by H. Toch (Chicago: Aldine Publishers, 1975), 181–205.

50. M. Weitman, "Extent of Criminal Activity, Sex and Varieties of Authoritarianism," *Psychological Reports* 13 (1963): 217–18.

51. B. Kay, "Can You Change This Image? A Report of Male-Female Differences in Attitudes toward the Police and Legal Institutions," *Police* 10 (1965): 30–32; and B. Kay, "Value Orientations as Reflected in Expressed Attitudes Are Associated with Ascribed Social Sex Roles," *Canadian Journal of Criminology and Corrections* 11 (1969): 193–97.

52. Kay, "Can You Change This Image?," p. 31.

53. G. P. Albert, "Comparative Look at Prisonization—Sex and Prison Culture," *Quarterly Journal of Correction* 1, no. 3 (1977): 29–34.

54. H. Sandhr and L. Irving, "Female Offenders and Marital Disorganization: An Aggressive and Retreatist Reaction," *International Journal of Criminology and Penology* 2 (1974): 35–42.

55. Maccoby and Jacklin, *Psychology of Sex Differences*, p. 114.

56. J. P. Stefanowicz and T. E. Hannum, "Ethical Risk-Taking and Sociopathy in Incarcerated Females," *Correctional Psychologist* 4 (1971): 138–52.

57. These are adjectives which are agreed upon by at least 50 percent of the officers as applying to females and males. The percentage agreements were then averaged to arrive at one percentage figure.

58. Adjectives are those which at least 55 percent of the officers agreed described one sex or the other.

3

Guarding Males and Females

A great deal of supervision involves reaction to perceptions of inmate behavior. Other supervision elements include how officers feel they should supervise, such as whether they should respond differently to male and female inmates under identical factual circumstances. An unsolicited example of an issue related to supervision was the officers' descriptions of differences between the supervision styles of male and female officers. Supervision differences are especially apparent to officers who have only worked with persons of their own sex and are then transferred to a facility that is staffed with a majority of opposite-sex officers.

There are very few studies which compare the supervision problems which may be present in institutions for men or women, although we can get some idea of gender-related supervision differences from the literature. Journalistic accounts describe female officers as treating women inmates like children, calling them "girls," and developing maternal styles of supervision.[1] It has also been pointed out that because of the small size of women's facilities, staff more frequently perceive their role as that of institutional "mothers," rather than custodians concerned only with enforcement of rules and regulations.[2] These characteristics of staff have been cited over and over again in descriptions of prisons for women. Some writers discuss the strong hold a personal staff-inmate relationship provides, since it involves more than formal punishment by including withdrawal of affection.[3]

Interestingly, current writers still identify one function of the correctional worker's job as meeting the emotional needs of women; as one writer put it, "inmates who could relate to staff would need fewer prison adjustments, such as the necessity of having pseudo-families."[4] Administrators also voice the belief that women inmates generally need more care than male inmates.

> I find that my whole management style had to change working at a female facility. . . . I have to be sensitive to the needs of females. They require more attention on a daily basis. Women are much more emotional and much more concerned about any problem, and all the key people here have to listen to those problems.[5]

Other writers characterize this same picture as one of psychological oppression which prevents independence, political consciousness, or personal maturation. The perceptions of women as children and as dependent and tractable persons are not exclusive to prisons; however, examples of this type of perspective in the prison literature are numerous.[6]

The literature on women correctional officers is relevant to women's prisons, since the majority of female officers are located in women's facilities. As discussed in the first chapter, studies show that female officers are generally more open to inmate problems, that inmates find them easier to talk to, and that female officers develop supportive relationships with inmates more readily than do male officers.[7] One study of a staff group in a women's prison also found that the women officers were more expressive about their feelings, and less callous towards the prisoners than the male officers.[8]

INSTITUTIONAL GOALS AND POLICIES

There is a substantial body of literature which discusses the impact of institutional goals on the correctional officers' jobs, both in the tasks they are expected to perform and the satisfaction they derive from their jobs.[9] Unfortunately, little research has been done on any differences which might exist between the current goals of men's and women's prisons. There are some studies which find that institutions for women subscribe to more treatment-oriented goals, partly because of differences in staff perceptions of male and female criminals. Women are seen by correctional workers as "less criminal" than male inmates. For instance, institutional policy is attributed to differential perceptions of male and female inmates, particularly to perceptions of men and women as being less dangerous and posing less of a security risk:

At the women's prison, inmates are allowed greater freedom than inmates at the men's prison. For example, women have relatively unrestricted movement in the correctional compound. Furthermore, the men's prison is often characterized by its more authoritarian system of control, whereas the women's prison has a more paternalistic control system. The basis of these differences in prison environments seems to be the difference in assumptions about how men and women prisoners should be treated. Male prisoners are viewed as more dangerous, with need for more stringent control, whereas women prisoners are construed as less harmful and in need of guidance.[10]

Women are also seen as childlike, according to researchers who have observed the tendency of correctional workers in facilities for women to refer to their inmates as girls.[11]

Differences in the perception of clients may be reflected in the goals of the institution. There is a fair amount of agreement in the literature that prisons for women are oriented towards treatment of the inmates as individuals rather than towards treating the inmate population as an aggregate or as a number of groups. Coercive control is also thought to be found less often in women's prisons. One study suggested that the reason for the two different control patterns in men's and women's prisons was the view that women were in prison for less serious crimes, along with the fact that male prisons are usually larger, hence, greater size and numbers force standardization and stricter control in order to insure the smooth operation of the facility.[12]

Another study discusses the different mechanisms for rule enforcement in male and female prisons. In this study, an institution with a disciplinary policy viewed as a "tolerance mechanism" is one that has "flexible rules," an attribute seen as prevalent in women's prisons:

A number of female correctional institutions seem to show a preference for this policy in order to maximize inmate-staff interaction as part of a philosophy of individual treatment. Similarly, as the degree of an institution's custodial mission increases, it might be expected that the staff will move closer to a "definite penalty" policy, by focusing on offense (not offender) characteristics. On the assumption that male institutions probably place a greater emphasis on custody and control, it is likely that these institutions levy more severe disciplinary sanctions.[13]

The author of the above study reviewed disciplinary boards' decisions in male and female prisons and reported that women received significantly less serious punishments for comparable offenses.[14]

There are contradictions in the literature regarding the differential treatment of men and women in prison. One group of researchers believes that because of small size, lack of anonymity, and disproportionately greater involvement by staff, women in prison feel oversupervised and oppressed by staff interest and control. Another group of researchers believes that because of more lenient control systems and more choices offered, women are subjected to less custodial control than that which is found in prisons for men. It should be noted that this controversy is similar to that relating to the question of whether a treatment institution is less or more oppressive than a custody institution. Because of the expanded interest of staff in the offender's life, some might argue that treatment facilities are actually more oppressive.

What evidence we have leads one to believe that institutions for women may be placed further towards the treatment end of the treatment-custody continuum. Studies dealing with male "treatment" prisons are helpful in identifying probable characteristics of a treatment orientation. For instance, Street, Vinter and Perrow, in their study of the goals of six different correctional facilities, found that as the goal of the institution moved from custody to treatment, inmates were perceived and treated on a more individual basis and that the staff had more varied tasks, more interdependent tasks, and were more often in conflict. They also found that as the goals of the institution moved towards treatment, staff's actions moved from actions "upon in-

mates" to "engagement of inmates."[15] Zald also found that institutions having either mixed goals or treatment goals had
higher levels of staff conflict than custodial institutions.[16]

Cressey has discussed the differences between the officers'
roles and responsibilities in treatment and custody institutions.[17]
Since the mandate of handling the inmate "individually" in a
treatment facility is hard to operationalize and evaluate, Cressey
writes that "contradictory directives for guards were even more
apparent in the treatment oriented prison than the custodially
oriented prison."[18] He also notes that it "was the duty of the
guards to respond therapeutically, to understand inmates and
their problems, to avoid being rigid or punitive,"[19] elements
which seem very consistent with the descriptions we have of
prisons for females. Other researchers have noted how the various characteristics of so-called treatment facilities, with their
emphases on clients and individualized attention, affect the officers' jobs. For instance, Grusky uncovered role conflict in an
institution where new treatment goals were introduced.[20]

Officers' Perceptions

In our interviews with officers, differences between institutions for men and women emerged fairly early. One difference
was in the perceived deemphasis of custodial features in the
prison regime in facilities for women. Officers complain that:

Very few people look upon females in the prison system as criminals.
Matter of fact, some administrators in the system don't even want you
to refer to them as inmates or prisoners.(I19-male)

They feel that because they're women, they should get a little extra, I
don't see why. I mean you do the same crime, you should get the same
time. (I21-male)

The administration is too busy trying to coddle the inmates here. Because they are females. When I first came to work here I was told you
are coming from a male facility and things are different than they are
here at BH. These are female inmates, they're going to be treated a lot
differently than you treated inmates at other jails. And I think that's

ridiculous. An inmate should be treated like an inmate no matter what jail they're incarcerated in. (I34-male)

Men seem to be treated like bad guys and women seem to be treated like kids. Those are major differences between the way I've seen male and female facilities operate. (P5-male)

As officers see it, the low custody emphasis in situations for women may be the cause of the architectural features of the institutions, the physical facilities and the way they are used.

It does seem that the facilities—at least outwardly—for women appear to be smaller and ... even the terminology seems a little different. Consistently at BH they refer to it as a housing unit rather than a cell block, and I think that frankly if you took men in and put men into it, it would all of a sudden be a cell block. Although the term "housing unit" is used in male facilities, it just isn't used as much. (P7-male)

The other physical difference that I see between the facilities is the fact that in the female surroundings they seem to lean more towards the femininity of the inmate by dealing with things that she would normally be in contact with, stoves and beauty parlors and things of this nature, whereas in the male facility those things are just limited to necessities. You would have some apparatus of eating food, a "dropper" or something of that nature and just the basics, a barber shop, for example. (I19-male)

Mentioned by officers much more frequently than physical or programmatic differences were differences in the deployment of rules and regulations. Most of the officers said that there were special rules invoked in dealing with women. Some officers felt the rules for women were more strict, but more frequently the officers believed that women were allowed special privileges. Even more common than the mention of special rules was the feeling that similar rules were enforced differently in male and female prisons.

Those few officers (less than 5 percent) who felt that the rules for women were stricter were located in the one co-correctional facility in the system. Their concern centered around the fact that women had more restrictions on their movement and needed to be escorted wherever they needed to go.

Women, almost everywhere they go, they have to be escorted by an officer. They don't have access to the grounds. A man who wants to come and see the nurse just has to come and reports to the officer at the desk. . . . A woman has to almost always be escorted . . . and that applies to the college program. The men go to the college program unescorted, the women go under escort and the escorting officer stays there. Almost any situation you want to draw a comparison to, the women's access to programs, etc., is more restricted than men's. (I9-female)

Those views were in the minority, however, and more officers felt that the rules present in facilities for women were disproportionately lenient (37 percent), especially in regard to the precautions taken in routine security measures.

Here . . . they don't take security seriously. Nothing is. They feel that an inmate shouldn't be leg-ironed because she's female, and I'm a firm believer that an inmate is an inmate—treat them all the same way. If one deserves leg irons, if they are a high security risk, they will go out in leg irons with me on an outside trip, anything of that nature. At GH nobody avoided any security questions. If you had a bad inmate going out you had three officers, two of them armed. Here at BH, it takes an Act of Congress to get two people armed taking a heavy time inmate and things like that. (I27-male)

I don't intend to beat anybody with a nightstick, but in a maximum security institution you should carry a nightstick, not as a weapon, but as a deterrent. If you carry one here, they, you know, they hit the ceiling. (I21-male)

About half of the officers believed that lax enforcement of existing rules in women's prisons was associated with a loss of control over inmate behavior.

A lot of things are mandatory in a male institution and it keeps men out of trouble as compared to this institution where things aren't mandatory. So, therefore, women have a lot of idle time on their hands and if they choose not to go to things, they just don't go. There's no follow up, there's no punishment for not attending things like there should be. (I18-female)

In a male institution, if you threatened an officer, if you hit a male officer, you were automatically locked. It doesn't happen here. In a male institution there are certain guidelines that inmates go by and they don't get out of line as much as they do here. Here officers are belittled, they're cursed at, they're dogged on a daily basis, o.k.? And there are no corrective measures that I've seen to bring about a change. (I18-female)

I found the rules and regulations to be pretty much the same ... they tended not to be as strictly adhered to with the women as they were with the men. It always seemed to me in retrospect that the women always got away with more than the men did. The rules and regulations were more strictly enforced with the men. I wouldn't say that there were more of them, but whatever there was was more strictly enforced. (P5-male)

Several of the officers saw the same situation, but felt it was changing.

The manner of enforcement may be a little different.... Let's put it this way, I think it was at one time, I don't think it is that much any longer. (P12-male)

I think ... because of the changeover of male supervisors coming in from high security jails, so they saw the way that it was in a high security jail, coming into this place, it's maximum security and they're trying to make it maximum security and they're trying to enact it. (I27-male)

As expected, size of the institution was a frequently mentioned difference by officers (90 percent). Although management problems created by the difference in size was not a major theme in officers' descriptions of the relative difficulties in supervising inmates, the intimacy which was present in smaller institutions was mentioned as an asset by some.

My sense is that any smaller facility has a more relaxed atmosphere, in the sense that people don't have to be watching so many people. There aren't so many inmates around. (P13-female)

Others discussed size in terms of how they had to change their supervision style when transferring from one prison to another.

The bottom line is numbers. When you're dealing with sixteen women on a corridor and when you're dealing with 100 men on a tier, your approach has to be different. The individual attention that every inmate received would be different. (11-male)

Lack of resources in women's prisons was not a predominant theme among the officers' descriptions; only 1 percent mentioned it at all. In the opinion of the staff, services and facilities for women are certainly no worse and might be a bit better than those for men. However, there are certain shortages and deficiencies that were perceived to cause problems. For instance, one administrator explained that because the state does not have adequate numbers of uniforms for women, this has resulted in an institutional response of allowing more personal clothing to be worn by female inmates. The amount of personal clothing allowed, in turn, was mentioned by some officers as an example of the less stringent security measures which make their job harder.

Whatever deficiencies were seen were explained by a number of officers in terms of the correctional system being set up for men, so that the needs of women inmates could not be understood and/or incorporated into the management of the system. As examples of this problem, women's uniforms are in short supply because of underestimated purchase orders; toilet tissue is constantly in short supply because women use more of it than men, but the central office allocates the same amount of equal numbers of men and women; and there are shortages of tampons and other hygiene items used by women because of underestimated purchase orders.

An interesting finding was that the officers did not believe that women needed more counseling help than males, and an overwhelming majority believed there were no gender-related differences in the need for psychiatric help (71 percent). A few officers even felt that males might need more psychiatric help than females because they were less likely to ask for such help and less willing to spontaneously discuss their problems.

Although there was no agreement among officers that women needed more counseling services than men, there seemed to be little disagreement about the women's greater need for medical care, even if only to deal with psychosomatic illnesses. Eighty percent of the officers felt women needed more medical services than the men.

Women have more psychosomatic illnesses than the men do, their heads hurt all the time, they have headaches, they have backaches, they have stomachaches, their abdomen hurts, they think they have an infected kidney, they think they have a bladder infection, they think they have everything. (I3-female)

Women do seem to have an awful lot of medical complaints and I believe that . . . women are seen generally more by some kind of medical staff than the men. . . . It could have to do with a lot of things in that women can express, I think they express their bad feelings through physical complaints and so consequently will make more complaints. Some of the women have had very hard lives and they've been physically abused, I just don't think they've had good maintenance health care, a lot of them. And then the drug abuse and the alcohol seems to be more devastating on women. (I9-female)

I don't know whether it's menstrual cramps or what, but they always got some kind of headache, stomachache, bodyaches here. A man, if he gets cut in the yard, he'll probably just fix it himself or won't make a big thing out of it. They gotta go to an outside hospital. . . . Women, I think . . . they're weaker in the mind, they're weaker in the body. (I35-male)

If a guy's hurt or breaks a leg or busts a finger or something, he'll go to the hospital and they're back walking on crutches two days later, you know, and still functioning. Whereas females, if she gets a torn hangnail, it's good for two days in bed. (I43-female)

Health care, I find, is greater than for men. The women tend to focus on their bodies a lot when they are incarcerated or they tend to want medical care that they haven't gotten on the outside or didn't bother to get when they were on the outside. Plus, just more things seem to go wrong, particularly in terms of gynecological problems, that the men don't have. (P8-female)

Summary of Goals and Policies

It was expected that many institutional characteristics would be perceived as different between institutions for men and women, and would be seen as affecting the work environment of the custodial officer. While 80 percent of the officers felt there were institutional differences, the only themes mentioned by a significant number of them related to rules (37 percent) and different enforcement patterns of rules (50 percent).

Less than 5 percent of the officers mentioned program differences, management-related differences due to the size of the institution, problems with being a single institution in a system or custodially relevant physical differences. This does not mean that these differences do not exist, but it does seem to indicate that the institutional differences are not perceived as being important or relevant to the officers in their daily activities.

INMATE TRAITS AND SUPERVISION

While the majority of officers recognized differences between male and female inmates, many of them did not necessarily affect the officers' role in supervision. It is clear, however, that some individual traits of inmates are perceived by the officers as making their job more difficult. We must caution again, that what we report here are only the perceptions of the officers—their descriptions of the trait differences between women and men have not been objectively measured or verified. In fact, some are recognizable as common stereotypes of female behavior. However, it is important to see what the officers see and understand the inmates as they understand them, in order for us to analyze supervision differences. The following, then, are some differences between male and female inmates that officers believe affect them.

Emotionality

Women were perceived as being more openly emotional than men. Fully 89 percent of the officers agreed with the statement that women were more emotional. The concept itself, or as used by the officers, had many components. In content analysis, the following elements of emotionality emerged:

1. Open displays of feelings through crying, laughing, hostile expression, and so on (87%);

2. Sharing among women of feelings and emotions, strong attachments between women (22%); and

3. Changeability of emotions without any observable reason, moodiness (5%).[21]

A large number of officers described the emotionality of women in terms of the first component—open displays of emotion.

But the women do get quite emotional at times, they show a lot of emotions like happiness, sadness, joy, when they see their kids; sometimes it's really quite touching. Sometimes their kids walk in that door and the mother bursts into tears and hugs them, you know, you don't see the men do that. (I8-female)

They tear up their rooms, they holler and scream and, you know, they show it; it's overt with a woman, with a man, it's not. (I15-female)

First time I ever had an inmate cry on my shoulders I was here two days. I never thought that'd happen in a jail. But you know it's something that you got to deal with in a female facility. Females cry all the time, and if they didn't cry, you'd think there was something wrong with them. I'd rather them cry it out than fight it out. I'll never knock a female, whether she be an inmate or a civilian, for crying, they're supposed to. (I27-male)

Here they cry in a hot second, if they flunked a high school exam, they cry. If they call home and there's no answer, they're in tears. (I27-male)

The males, they're more easier to work with in that they're not emotional about a lot of things. And when you work with the women, you know, you see ten or fifteen of them a day, you're almost emotionally drained because they have presented so many emotions to you. (P4-male)

As officers see it, one difficulty with emotionality is that the emotion displayed by the inmate may translate into hostility directed towards the officer.

When you find him guilty of an infraction of the rules and mete out a certain kind of punishment, the male inmate won't like it, but he'll walk out of the room and go handle his punishment. The female will scream and yell that she's being treated unjustly and it's not fair and she didn't do it.... I've seen females when they get bad news from the parole board, they get extremely hostile about the bad news; when they get no for an answer, they get hostile and loud, a man won't like it, but he'll just shake his head and grumble and walk away. (I12-male)

If a ... male inmate disagrees with a rule, more often than not he will accept what you say and deal with it later ... where a female will usually just act out on you. She will use foul language or demand certain things from you, say "that answer ain't good enough for me, I want to see a supervisor" ... that type of yelling. (I24-male)

When officers were asked if females "acted out" more than male inmates, an overwhelming majority said they did (85 percent). Acting out is a somewhat undefined term, but the officers seemed to be very clear on the meaning they assigned to the term. The most frequently given descriptions of acting-out behavior by women relate to expressive emotionality. Women were described as frequently having tantrums or outbursts of anger in which they engage in verbal assaults on officers. Of those who perceived women to act out more than men, roughly 60 percent described some episode of untrammeled abuse.

Hysteria, verbal profanity ... stand right in your face and just tell you right off. (I19-male)

They become verbally abusive, physically abusive ... cause a disturbance, whatever. (I39-female)

Any incident created more disturbance with the women than it did with the men—always. (P5-male)

Very closely connected to the expressivity theme is the perception that woman have a "shorter fuse," that it takes less stimulation or provocation for a woman to express herself in an emotional way.

They'll become hysterical, saying you're destroying their dignity or some such thing in a strip search, a male will accept that more readily I think, although they don't particularly care for it either. (I38-female)

I think they lose their temper much easier, fly off the handle more easily, they have less control of themselves in any given situation, they get extremely upset extremely quick. (I12-male)

Because women were adjudged less likely to hide emotions, officers felt they had to watch what they said to female inmates and to be more sensitive to how a woman was likely to react to them.

I can say things to males that I can't say to females because of the emotionality factor.... They're delicate. There's a fear of breaking their hearts. Don't want to be the one to tip over the applecart. (I11-male)

Well, the female inmates are much more critically handled than the male inmates. Every time you deal with a female, you have to be very careful and selective of your words because something that you can tell a male inmate, you know, "come on" or "hop along" or "clear the corridor" and if you tell that to females, you may very well have a hairpulling contest. (I19-male)

It is clear from the above accounts that officers, especially male officers, were used to dealing with inmates in a brusque, authoritarian style in maximum security prisons for men. (This is consistent with the findings from the literature survey presented in chapter 1.) These officers were surprised and dismayed when women inmates reacted violently to the same management style that the officer had been using with no problem up to the transfer.

Other elements of emotionality are by-products of the perceived readiness for and display of emotions. The first corollary is the sense that one must deal with the ever-present moodiness of inmates and the emotional lability of settings that contain women.

And they have that thing that comes along every month that makes them irritable and puts them in an ugly mood. (I2-female)

Somehow they wake up in the morning moody, some of them won't even get themselves together, they'll just be negative until they get up, take a shower, get some coffee.... When they get up in the morning, they curse you out, call you all kinds of names, but by 9:30 they will apologize, "I'm sorry I didn't feel too good this morning." (I36-male)

Men seem to be more stable than women. One woman can be at a high one day and the next day she can be very low, and the men generally you get one man and he's generally that way most of the time unless something comes up, you know, to push him over the edge. But generally, they're the same way the whole time you know them. The women go up and down. (P4-male)

Women are also seen as becoming more emotionally involved with each other, whether it be merely through expressing affection or becoming actively involved in each other's problems. This involvement often has undesirable consequences for the officer, since an officer may be interacting with one inmate and suddenly find himself or herself dealing not only with that individual but also with a number of the inmate's friends.

Women can hug and show expression to each other but the public doesn't accept men hugging and showing affection to men. (P6-male)

The women are more likely to form emotional attachments which are not necessarily stable, but they are more emotional than the males. Males tend to—they'll have a friend maybe, but the women will go to the family systems, and call each other by pet names and those kind of things, as opposed to males. (P8-female)

One of the females in the group may be having an emotional problem, may be having a physical problem, a family problem, that's got her all upset and all her friends would congregate around her to give her sympathy and console her, to give her direction, to give her moral support, whatever, and an officer, unknown to him what's going on ... would say "o.k., let's break it up and move along," and right away something will develop because they will feel that this is an attack upon this person that's having the problem.... They would become very abrasive to that officer and the degree of it would depend on the degree of emotional involvement of the group. (I19-male)

The more empathy occurs, the less likely you're able to speak to one woman at a time because it gets to be like one big family and you can't do something which they believe is going to hurt someone in the family, you know, without them getting involved, so in that sense, it makes it harder. (P5-male)

Quite a large number of our sample of officers (47 percent) were not willing to state categorically that women were more emotional than men, but rather, stressed the tendency of male inmates to suppress emotion behind a "tough guy" or "macho" facade.

Men cover up with a tough guy pose, women cry. (I5-male)

The males tend to hide it like they do at home because it's not a mannish thing to do. (I8-female)

Women get emotional over bad news, men work it out in the gym. (I12-male)

Males hide their emotions. I believe they are emotional, but they don't cry or nothin'. (I37-male)

Men will hold that macho image, you know, "I'm not going to cry for nothing," but you know just by looking at them that they want to. (I41-female)

I think men internalize an awful lot more than they need to and more of that than woman do. And so you don't see outside, but the emotion is there. It's just the expression of it is hidden. (P2-female)

Officers described a fight-flight syndrome in men. They felt that men coped with their emotion by withdrawal, through displaced physical activity, or through physical attacks on others.

Men either withdraw or get physically aggressive. Most of the men would kind of just withdraw for a couple weeks and gradually come out of it. (I42-male)

If it gets too much it's like they hit on a wall or slam doors or throw things in their rooms where they don't think anybody sees them. (I15-female)

If they blow, it may be a few hours, it may be a few days, it may come out as a fight with another inmate, who knows? A lot more of the men are athletically inclined, they play basketball, they lift weights, and some of the hostility, if that's possible, I think, goes into the physical stuff. (I12-male)

I had one that I had never had a problem with and I came in one day and he said "Lock me up" and I looked at him and said "why?," and he said "I can't tell you." So I took him up to "seg" myself ... and he finally told me that he had read in the newspaper that his daughter was in a fire so I knew he was holding all this in and I said, "Why don't you let it all out?" and he said, "I can't let it out down there that's why I want to go up here, because up here I can be locked away and I can sit down and just think and if I feel like crying I can cry, but in front of all these other guys, I can't." (I41-female)

Several different interpretations were placed on the expressive emotionality of women. While 5 percent of the officers who believed women were more emotional highlighted physical or biological causes (such as stress factors or lack of control), others in the group (10 percent) saw more instrumental qualities in the women's behavior (a call for help, desire for attention, or attempts at manipulation through provocation, intimidation, or sympathy).

What happens I think is the female gets caught up in the emotion and there's no cut off point, it just keeps ... the adrenalin just keeps rising and, uh, they become much more involved. (I43-female)

Sure, women will do it more, that's why they live longer. ... A woman's stress factor is twice that of all others and when you relieve the stress through crying, screaming, you live longer. (I7-male)

I have always been under the impression that women do that in the hopes that you will retaliate by doing something stupid, either lowering yourself to their level, which many officers do by just returning with profanity, or by even touching them, pushing them away and telling them to go to their unit, which right away they pick up as an assault or some form of harassment. (I19-male)

Women do that for the attention because they're more afraid. Jail is, believe me, a tough place. It's tough on them and they do this for more attention. I think it's a call for help, like last week, one of the inmates was sick, but then another inmate started yelling that she's gonna cut up now. It's only to get attention. (I35-male)

They often use it as a technique, I seem to think, especially to male officers who they really feel don't care for them, who think they are less acceptable. And I think they use verbal abuse and some rough language to shock them. (I9-female)

Sometimes they get tantrums, they get fits of rage, when it's not really necessary, because this is the way they can get attention. (I29-female)

I don't know whether that's not looking for sympathy. I know I have women on disciplinary hearings, and I see a lot of tears. I don't know if the emotions they display here are all real. (I6-male)

You know my feeling about the loud, aggressive screaming and yelling by the women. I don't attribute it to emotionality. It's a front. (P7-male)

It is obvious that the display of emotions by female inmates is a salient issue for officers supervising women, but that officers' interpretations of these expressed emotions are varied.

Demands and Complaints

We recall that 71 percent of the total sample of officers felt that women complained more frequently than males (Table 3). In the officers' descriptions, a theme emerged which may be characterized as a lack of prioritizing of issues. About 25 percent of the officers saw women as tending to become upset or to be extremely demanding about "little things." As the majority of the officers see it, female inmates are just as demanding or complain just as vociferously about something trivial as about something more important. This may relate to the "shorter fuse" of women as discussed in the section on emotionality, or it may be that women do not prioritize concerns in the same manner as males. The officers also implied that when men did demand or complain, they were taken more seriously.

I think smaller things affect them more ... making something out of nothing. (I1-male)

Women complain a lot more than the males. Like, uh, little things. If they have a headache, they act like they're going to go crazy and they want to see a nurse or a doctor for everything and they get very loud if you don't run and get them what they want. (I17-female)

Women will complain about everything, men will wait for something serious or unjust. (I21-male)

The women complained about everything and always did it vociferously. It made no difference to them if they were complaining about staff members beating them up as opposed to seeing a cockroach running across the floor ... whereas the men seemed to do things differently. The nature of their complaints would be more towards serious matters, less towards the frivolous kind of thing and the intensity would vary. The more serious the complaint, the more intense would be their response to it. (P5-male)

Women will complain about a lot more things that are trivial. . . . Everything seems to be a monumental problem, o.k.? Rather than sitting down and really looking at those problems that are monumental and those problems that are really insignificant, the women don't prioritize. (P12-male)

In addition to facing an indiscriminate range of complaints and demands, some of the officers (37 percent) felt they had to deal with a greater amount of unreasonableness about what the inmates wanted and the immediacy with which they wanted it.

They'd want to know if there were movies tonight and I'd say "I have to check, I'm not sure." If you said this to men, they'd say "o.k., let me know when you find out." Now the women, they say "well, I want to know." They want to know that instant. They don't have the patience. (I4-female)

Everything "right now," everything is an emergency and "I want it right now." Males are more than willing to write a letter or you could tell an inmate to wait two weeks; here they don't want to wait two hours. (I37-male)

An observation less agreed upon, but still mentioned by some officers (about 17 percent), was that women are more demanding and complain more about personal grievances, whereas men demand redress or complain about problems that relate to the institution or to many inmates.

I feel that women are more self centered, that they ask for more. (I13-male)

They complain when it comes to what they are allowed . . . like cosmetics. (I5-male)

Men and women are demanding about different things. Women demand more personal things. (I42-male)

I'd put it this way. Women are more demanding personally—medical attention, clothes, hygiene needs, where the men are more demanding, uh, "where is my money for my job?," things that a man would get from the institution. (I43-female)

Again, it goes back to the women want more things that benefit them personally and the males want institutional or departmental changes. (I42-male)

This perception may be reflecting women's relative lack of "politicalization" or awareness of the power of group demands, something that is discussed in the next chapter. It should be noted that the perception of women being self-centered runs contrary to an earlier perception that women were more emotionally involved in each other's problems. It may be that officers perceive personal concerns of women as trivial and self-centered, while the male concerns, which may be more "acceptable" to officers, and also may carry the power of a group, garner more respect from officers.

Women inmates were also perceived to demand more attention from the officers (this need for attention was previously mentioned as a reason for open emotionality).

Female inmates are much more demanding of your time. . . . Male inmates tend to be more business. (I8-female)

They demand attention . . . use little problems to get attention. (I12-male)

They want constant attention and it's kind of hard when you're dealing with sixty women to give each one individual constant attention. (I34-male)

To be sure, there were some officers who saw no differences in the types of complaints or demands from male and female inmates. These officers saw men and women as tending to voice similar complaints and as calling for comparably unreasonable levels of service.

They run pretty much the same. Looking for a better job or a special privilege. (16-male)

No matter what you do or how you do it and no matter how hard you try you absolutely cannot please people in prison. (13-female)

There were a few officers, however, who cited mitigating circumstances and believed that women complained more because they had less.

An inmate is demanding because she has nowhere else to go. (140-female)

I also think that is because they are usually in more restrictive settings and have to ask for more than men do. (19-female)

Males are not as demanding, because, frankly speaking, in the facility that I was in, they got more than the females in this facility. (128-female)

Other officers had another explanation which involved the idea that women had a more difficult time adjusting to prison and consequently felt entitled to supports and special privileges.

I think a male inmate can more easily adapt himself to a lack of privileges and the confining nature of a correctional facility where a female is not as quickly or readily adaptable to a controlled type atmosphere.... Maybe the male inmate is more institutionalized. (110-male)

They will not accept the fact that they are incarcerated in a penal institution. They will not accept the fact that certain privileges that you might have on the street have been taken away. I think they refuse to accept the fact that they are not on the street. It's harder for them to do time and I don't know whose fault that is, whether it's their fault or the system. (112-male)

Manipulation

Sixty-two percent of the officers who were interviewed felt women were more manipulative than men. Among both these officers and those who felt men and women were equally manipulative, there was a perception that women and men used different manipulation techniques. Of the techniques perceived to be unique to women, the one mentioned most frequently was that women used "female charms" to influence male officers (36 percent).

They use flattery, scanty dressing. . . . There's always a payoff. (I11-male)

. . . try to use their sex, being nice. They can be very lovable when they want something. . . . They try to work you. (I16-male)

It's their female ways, words, seductive ways to get what they want. (I20-male)

With a male officer, they'll try compliments, they'll dress better if the male officer is present, they'll try to use their female lures to try to gain his confidence that way. It may be innocent, but it also could be that they want something. Women play much more on your emotions . . . "I'm a poor helpless female and you're a strong male." (I42-male)

At times the manipulation may take on sexual connotations. Or at least, especially female inmates to male employees, the female inmate will come on as the weak woman and try to be manipulative that way. (P12-male)

Among the techniques attributed to inmates of both sexes, one noted by many officers was the technique of going from officer to officer until the desired answer was received.

First, they'll ask one officer about doing it, then they'll go to another officer and then they'll figure out that neither one of you are going to bend and they'll get somebody that will bend. (I27-male)

In other words, if you get a negative answer out of one, they leave the area without saying anything. They can go and ask the other officer and get a positive answer. Females are slicker, they do it with more finesse. (143-female)

Officers perceive both sexes as currying favors through help-fulness and/or friendliness, but there was a feeling that men were more subtle and patient in carrying out this enterprise.

Males are more successful in "gaming you" by doing things for you. . . . Women won't follow through . . . won't work on it for a long time. (125-male)

They try to use friendship to get you to do a favor for them. Men will try to scheme you too, but they'll take a longer time at it. (137-male)

The men are more cleverly manipulative. It takes longer, I found, to tell when the male is manipulating you. They're lower key about it. (P8-female)

The charge is that what women lack in patience, they make up for in imagination. Several officers mentioned that a favorite technique of women was the use of long, involved stories to manipulate the officers into giving them special privileges. In-terestingly, these descriptions are similar to those listed earlier of officers who complained that women did not admit wrong-doing, but tended to "explain away" their actions.

They'll try to manipulate you with, you know, pity. Women will tend to ask for favors from officers and counselors for special phone calls. "I just heard that my daughter flunked her class." They'll dream up excuses as to why they have to call home and it might end up that they're really just homesick and they want to talk to somebody at home. (18-female)

They use long stories with details to get what they want. (113-male)

It's like they tell you about their aches and pains and the doctors and the nurses not helping. Anything they try to use it for extra privileges, everything is to gain. (115-female)

One interesting alleged difference was that males tend to in-fluence officers through other inmates, whereas women concen-trated their efforts on influencing the officers directly.

Men have a tendency to manipulate the weaker men in the facility, to get sexual favors or commissary buys, things of that nature. (I34-male)

Males manipulate among themselves, but females try to manipulate officers more. (I22-female)

Males did it by other inmates. They'd get another inmate. Let's say one inmate is one of your good workers, o.k.? If he couldn't get what he wanted from you, he would get his friend, who's a good worker, and usually got a little bit something extra, a different privilege, and tell him to do it. They would do it like that. (I27-male)

Unpredictability

About 64 percent of the officers believed women were more unpredictable than men. One theme involved the officers' ability to sense when something was going to happen. Evidently, when working with males, there is a feeling of continuity or stability and a higher probability that the officers may feel forewarned when something is about to "jump off."

Males, when they are coming at you, you can see it, females will say "yes, yes" and go out the door and throw something. (I32-male)

I've been on this job awhile now and you get this sense of when something's going to go off. I have it here too. It's just that in a male joint, you know when you come in to work that something just doesn't seem right, you feel something. Here, things are normal one minute and then the next minute, the inmate is doing a complete turnabout and in that sense she's very unpredictable. You never know what to expect from a female inmate. (I34-male)

Part of the reason for this alleged unpredictability may be the perceived moodiness of women which was discussed in an earlier section. Women are also regarded as being more unpredictable because they are more impulsive.

Women do things without thinking. (I8-female)

They're very spontaneous. (I20-male)

They do things on the spur of the moment. (I25-male)

Openness

More positively valued was the perception that women were more open in sharing their problems. Sixty-two percent of the officers interviewed perceived women as more likely than males to discuss personal problems.

Men will sit in their cell bumping their head against the wall, but a woman wants you to solve her problems. (I21-male)

Men will take their problems to their cell, close the door and read a book, whatever. But women will take theirs out and share it, display it, let everybody see what was bothering them. (I36-male)

Females are more open in relation to their children or if they're having a problem, their children are sick or one of their parents is sick, they express that more than a male would. (I22-female)

According to the officers, the content of problems legitimately discussed by men and women diverges, and the differences seem consistent with our previous finding that women are perceived to complain about many types of personal difficulties in contrast to the male tendency to be more concerned with institutional problems and grievances.

It seems that the males have more institutional problems or problems that they think are problems. Females seem to have more personal problems. (I2-female)

They seem to have more personal problems. Maybe that's because they have more interest in children outside and family. Men don't seem to really worry too much about families outside. (I6-male)

The officers felt that women had a larger number and variety of problems, personal and otherwise. The problem most frequently singled out by the officers was that of abandonment by the women's families and separation from children.

They don't have as many people supporting them while they are in jail, you know, there will be some male inmates who have relatives, three or four girlfriends, wife and all that coming, where the women don't have as many. It's much more difficult for women with children because their children are apt to be in foster situations or in poor family situations whereas an awful lot of the men have quite traditional family settings with wives who take care of the children. (I9-female)

Men always seem to have good community support. They always have someone who is coming to them, women who come to them, their wives, their mothers, their sisters, their families, seem to be very attentive. And women, on the other hand, very few women have good community support. They have very few husbands coming to visit. (I3-female)

Women are picked up by the criminal justice system, find themselves all of a sudden in jail, and where are the kids? And so many of the men have a woman who still cares for them and hasn't rejected them because they're in prison.... They have children and ... all of a sudden it hits them that maybe they should be with their kids doing what they're supposed to do ... and they really have an awful time. (P1-female)

One explanation of why men were less open about their personal lives had to do with the assumption that male inmates needed to erect a stoic, tough, "macho" facade. Expressing problems is similar in some regards to expressing emotions, since it puts the individual in a vulnerable situation. No doubt it is due to these similarities that the officers' descriptions here parallel those used earlier to characterize the male tendency to hide emotion.

I've observed men in work release who were having some serious problems, the air of bravado still carried through. They wouldn't discuss their problems with the counselor, never mind with other inmates. (P8-female)

I think the males tend to withhold a lot. Males have to present a macho figure whether they want to or not. I mean it's forced on a male inmate. They have to whether they can back it up or not. (I42-female)

I think they feel that things aren't supposed to bug them, they're supposed to be tough all the time even though they're not. (I8-female)

Somewhat surprising was the finding that although officers experience the women to be more open with their problems, they did not perceive women as any easier than the men to "get to know." Only 36 percent of the officers felt women were easier to become relatively intimate with. The majority of officers felt they didn't know any inmate very well, and furthermore they didn't desire any personal knowledge or intimacy with them. This idea becomes important later when officers discuss their personal preferences as to whom they would rather supervise.

Homosexuality

Our concern with prison homosexuality was limited to whether it causes problems for officers and whether there are differences in the number or nature of the problems caused by female inmate homosexuality as compared to homosexuality in prisons for males. The data show that 60 percent of the officers felt they experienced greater problems in a female facility due to homosexual activities. Although this was not significantly different from the 40 percent who did not believe that greater problems were caused by female homosexuality, the officers described differences in how this behavior was manifested.

Both male and female homosexuality were seen as likely to cause jealousy and fights.

If two girls are living together and . . . if they are homosexual and they're each other's lovers and they have a fight . . . they're always screaming and yelling and it leads to fights and it causes a lot of problems. (I35-male)

Even married women in jail establish a homosexual relationship in jail and then when the husband comes up and she has a visit or something, the "butch" gets jealous, beats her up when she gets back or before she goes so she can't go. (I39-female)

One problem described was specific to female prisons. The officers felt that the frequency and openness with which homosexuality is practiced in women's prisons make it impossible to ignore, and that as a result, the officer as enforcer of prison rules is placed in a difficult position.

You don't want them on the same floor because they'll sit and kiss and hug all day long and this is supposed to be a prison, right? They turn it into a lover's paradise by having the lover here and the lover there; they're in the shower together, they're in the kitchen together, they're on the couch together, and you, as the officer, have to come between them all the time. (I18-female)

It's a big problem because when the officer catches them in a compromising position, the officer has to write them up; what they claim is that the officers are as queer as they are and they attack the officers' credibility. And if it's a male officer, in some cases they will offer sexual favors to the male not to turn them in or they'll tell the male that you had no business being here and they will address a court order that has already been moved upon that the officer had not given his name out or yelling that a man was on the unit or things of this nature. (I19-male)

If I was to enforce every rule on homosexuality here as far as holding hands or kissing or hugging or anything like that, I would need three secretaries to write the reports. (I27-male)

You know, if you decide that all of that stuff is bad and you want to stop it, well you're going to have a lot of problems, and they do. They have a lot of problems when they try to stop that.... You don't want touching, you don't want kissing ...so one of two things happens. If you really enforce not letting those things happen, if you really enforced it, I think you get a tremendous violent response and if you let sensuality exist ...then the problems of that would be a policy decision and the problem it causes is usually the staff does not agree with you and they feel that it should be knocked off. (P5-male)

According to officers, problems of homosexuality in male prisons are more likely to be related to the potential they hold for overt violence or coercion.

If a male inmate has another male inmate that is his "woman," he will fight to protect that "women" and he'd want to kill anyone that wanted to touch him. They're very possessive about their "wife" or whatever you want to call them and they're more physical about it than the women. (I8-female)

In a male facility, it would be a lot more serious.... When there is a problem, it is more serious in the male facility. Pipings or stabbings over love triangles or whatever, you find a lot more of that. (I23-male)

In the male institution when you have a homosexual, he's under the threat of being raped, where in the female institution you don't have that danger.... Usually homosexual relationships in a male institution are for protection, he needs someone to protect him and this is what he's got to do to get it. (I24-male)

With the males, usually it requires the man to be beat because he didn't give up anything and he took a beating for it and there was usually some type of internal damage to him. Female facilities, I have never seen a downright nasty homosexual act at this facility, but I have read reports that there have been. (I27-male)

If it appears to officers that the male prison is a more violent environment than the women's facility, this does not mean that they believed women did not feel intimidated or felt a need to protect themselves. It was surprising how many officers perceived the female homosexual role of "stud" as primarily a protective device. Furthermore, a number of officers believed that many ostensibly homosexual relationships were, in reality, links between friends who used the subcultural roles of "stud" and "femme" to protect the weaker of the two inmates.

Say you have two friends that are very close. One might be more assertive than the other and she feels she has to protect her friend. (I8-female)

If they play the mannish role, they protect someone else that needs it ...because they won't have to worry about anyone stealing anything, wouldn't have to worry about anyone hitting them, taking their food or jewelry. (I4-female)

They come in and they feel they have to give off a certain aura of strength to keep others off them. (I15-female)

As a cover in order not to be picked on, they take on the masculine role. (I18-female)

The officers believed, as did the prison researchers we have cited, that women engage in homosexual relationships for reasons that are not only sexual, but related to the possibility that women need emotional attachments more than males, or become more deeply involved in platonic relationships with members of their own sex.

I think women need emotional ties more than men do. And I think women can relate to each other more than men can in an emotional type of way, so I find more homosexuality among women than I've ever seen in a male prison. (I24-male)

It's hard to distinguish homosexuality with the women. I mean it's there, but again it's the emotional ties that the women have, they're more emotionally tied to each other and more loving than men and they can kiss and hold hands or something and I don't really consider it to be a lesbian experience.... Women seem to be much more closer together and it seems to be more prevalent with females than it is with males. (P4-male)

The women ... formed stronger relationships with each other than the men ever did. Men tended to talk about each other as acquaintances, where women tended to talk about each other as friends within the institution. The bonds were a lot more close than they were with the men or appear to be. The sexual relationships between women as well as the friendly relationships were a lot stronger with the women than with the men. The men, sexually, tended to rip each other off, the women, sexually, tended to care for each other and really feel for each other so the emotional bonds were stronger and the bonds of friendship were stronger. (P5-male)

It's more just to be able to touch somebody, sit close to somebody. And a lot of that, I think, is acceptable between females.... The ties they form in here are much stronger. (P8-female)

Leaders and Inmate Organization

As discussed previously, officers felt that men and women approached institutional issues and grievances differently. While women tended to focus on smaller issues and were more likely to take an individualistic approach, the men were more likely to organize and confront the administration en masse. Sixty-two percent of the officers believed that women were less likely to organize in the sense of writing petitions or forming protest groups. The officers were also asked whether leaders were less likely to emerge among women, and 64 percent of them said they believed that to be the case.

Males are much more quick to organize. Men tend to, if there's a cause, want to go along, want to be part of the system that they're involved in . . . they don't want to show a loss of faith. . . . They feel that if someone doesn't go along, well, then they'll deal with that someone, they will consider that person untrustworthy, they might even consider that person a "rat." And there's a fear of being a "rat" in prison, as witness Attica. Quite a few people with two or three months to go were caught up in the yard and had to go along. I think women tend to more go their own way, you know, "you deal with that, it's not my problem." (I24-male)

The men have a greater tendency to organize and to study and to check into their legal aspects. The women do it, but they push for petty things. They don't push for the things that would make the place run better. (I18-female)

Men organize better. I believe men say they're gonna do something, they're gonna get 10 guys to riot, men will do it and they'll go through with it. . . . Men are more aggressive, they know they've been wronged, they're gonna organize. . . . Women do it on an individual basis, to writing the letters to lawyers, writing the letters to the superintendent, to [state capital]. (I35-male)

I guess the men acted in a more organized way I would say; but not that the women acted one at a time, the men just organized it and orchestrated it better. (P5-male)

In explaining the difference, the officers hypothesized that women are more individualistic, selfish, and self-centered, and that they find it difficult to submit to compromise for the sake of group goals and solidarity.

Women are selfish and will not work as a group, they'll work against each other. (P10-male)

There's more unity among men; every woman is striving to prove something or out for themselves, not concerned with the next problem. (I34-male)

Men realize there's strength in numbers; women are out for what they can get. They'll question everything, men go along for the ride. (I32-male)

The women themselves can't get together. If there were twenty, there would be four different ideas and four different groups, and whereas the men will develop a mutual goal if it's important. (I19-male)

As officers see it, women may congregate as small groups of intimates, while men tend to organize into larger social groupings with formal leadership, especially by race.

Males organize in race groups ... in larger groups. (I16-male)

With women here there is no leader, they all think they're leaders. In a male institution, there might be a Muslim clique, an Italian clique, a farmer clique, an Irish clique, a Sunni Muslim clique and they each one will have a leader, where here they all got their own clique. They do not band together for anything. (I37-male)

Women tend to have their own little peer groups more than the men do.... It's more of a racial thing with men.... I found that men congregate only racially. (I42-female)

Officers' responses indicate that women's associations tend to be personal instead of impersonal, individual instead of organized, and emotional instead of utilitarian; they feel that among women there is more involvement, but that support tends to be given in an unorganized, individual manner. The officers also felt that while women are concerned with issues affecting them as individuals, men are more apt to address issues of common concern to them as a group.

The reasons given for the differences between men and women are varied. Most officers suggest that differences emerge from the different socialization patterns of men and women. Some officers refer to experiences men have with large groups such as unions and the army, as compared to the women's traditional role in society as dependents isolated in homes. A few officers suggested that the loyalty of male inmates to groups is often fear inspired, citing both the fear of other groups and the fear of members of one's own group should one not "go along with the program."

According to 64 percent of the officers, one was less likely to find leaders among women. Some officers charged that all inmates wanted to be leaders, and an equal number said that no female aspired to be a leader. Leaders among men were perceived to be more constructive and less transitory than female leaders. Male leaders were also seen to have more control over the behavior of their followers, and more likely to be associated with a particular identifiable and permanent group.

Compliance

In the same way that females tend to be seen as resistant to following inmate-led direction, they are also seen as less likely to follow officer supervision. Sixty-seven percent of the officers believed they had greater difficulty in securing compliance from women. Both male and female officers felt that women were less likely to follow orders, although women officers were slightly more likely to report this difference than were male officers (78 percent of the female officers as compared to 63 percent of male officers). The officers described women as questioning their orders more often, "giving them lip," and needing constant supervision to get a task done.

Officers' explanations of why women tend not to follow orders as readily as male inmates include the idea that women do not accept the "fact" of their imprisonment, a concept discussed in previous sections. The premise was that women show less respect for authority and demand better treatment than is customarily available in a prison environment. As a result, women are seen as not complying with orders or reacting resentfully to the way in which orders are given.

They're very sensitive to being treated like ladies and not being pushed around. The men just kind of took that for granted. Women do not.

They'll complain if they feel someone has treated them discourteously. (P8-female)

I think because your female inmates recognize that all your legal institutions and your courts all deal very favorably with female inmates because they're special. You know, I feel women are special too, o.k.? It's been my upbringing, but you can't have the best of both worlds. (I19-male)

Many officers described male inmates as carrying out their assignments without the officers needing to tell them what to do. One female officer offered an intriguing explanation for their perceived difference. She observed that because of the macho image, males hate to be told by women officers what to do; therefore, they complete their tasks before being given the command, in order to preserve their dignity.

Males do not like to be told by females what to do so they will more or less do what they have to do, without, you know, they don't want you to speak on it. Like if you're taking them to chow, you know, you don't have to tell them to get to the right because they don't want you to open your mouth so they're going to be to the right. (I22-female)

It seems logical that it would also be damaging to a male's ego to have a male officer tell him what to do, so this same explanation may apply more generally to why officers seem to have less "trouble" with male inmates.

Assaultiveness

Although there were not statistically significant differences in the officers' perceptions of the frequency of assaults by men and women on other inmates or against officers, we will examine these responses because, according to their descriptions, assaults by men and women tended to manifest themselves in very different forms. Thus, the same adjective seems to have been used to describe different patterns of behavior.

First, officers perceived differences in the spontaneity and frequency of attacks; women were perceived to fight more readily over minor issues. Second, differences were also described in the degree or intensity of assaults, with women's assaultiveness being perceived as relatively less dangerous, but as relatively more troublesome. Ironically, officers believed that women's assaults were more "vicious" because of the untrammeled, out-of-control, "no holds barred" flavor to the women's fighting.

Women like to fight and they'll fight more readily, more easily and for lesser reasons than the men will. (I3-female)

I think that with the women, it's more frequent . . . it's more spontaneous. In other words, I think that . . . most of the assaults that took place were unplanned, they were spontaneous situations and the women just lashed out. If it was another inmate or staff, all the better. But the men tended to, if you wanted to call that part of control, were more controlled in that sense, you know, they would go back and fester. The men, I think, were more like Doberman pinschers, the way they operate. (P5-male)

I think due to the emotionality and the way of dealing with problems, the women, in terms of violence, are more spontaneous. The men are a lot more calculating and planned, and subsequently will work it so that it's done when no one else is around. (P12-male)

Females argue a lot and they fight with each other more than men, but men are more harmful when they really go after someone. They, like you say, "cut your throat," right? And females tend to handfight or use a chair or something . . . but males go more for hurting each other very bad. They don't fight that much, but when they do, it's serious. (I17-female)

Men do not fight as often as women, but when they do fight, it is usually to try to seriously injure one another. It's not a slapping contest or pulling hair type of thing. When they do this, they're out for blood. So fights that I have been involved in, that I have separated, men will tend to separate quicker because they know that danger between the two of them is there. It's not just a thing, it could lead to other things later on. So I think that sometimes the men will separate; they don't want to show that they will, but they, in a sense, require you to use less force. They will separate. (I24-male)

Women are harder to deal with as far as assaults. They're vicious, they will scratch you. Instead of giving you a good punch, they will scratch you, they will cut you, they will do anything they can to hurt you. Men, when they say they're gonna knock you out, they'll give you a beating like you never got before in your life, but you can deal with that because they're not there to really scratch you, harm you, scar you; they'll punch you and they'll make a bruise and they may break a bone. Usually though they'll leave no marks, a female will leave marks, I'd never been bitten till I got here. (I27-male)

Women are very dirty fighters, they scratch, pull hair; men, well, they do pick up weapons, I can't say they don't do that, but nine times out of ten they fight, if there is such a thing. . . . It's still gonna be bloody, but it's not a case where, unless it's really something that they planned that they're going to have something to fight with, nine times out of ten I can go out there and stop it. But with the women, you'd have to have six officers to stop a fight. (I41-female)

Women are a lot more aggressive, o.k.? If a female gets mad at you, she'll scratch your eyes out, pull your hair, she'll rip your shirt off, anything that a female would do when they get emotionally mad, o.k.? If a guy gets mad at ya, he's going to cuss at ya, he might hit ya, but he'll usually walk away. (I43-female)

A few offi . . . suggested that it could often be the case that female inmates were not directing their violence at the officer, but rather, were trying to get at another inmate and the officer happened to "get in the way."

Officers believed that women tended to fight openly or to advertise their conflicts, while men planned for and concealed their fighting.

Women tend to showboat, men don't. Like even here if a girl was going to fight, quite often she'd wait until she got in the messhall so that all the girls were around, not just three or four girls on her unit. Where men will, at least from what little I've observed here and what I know the male officers have said, they'll tend to get you later, on the side of the building and that way nobody . . . goes to "lock." We've had a couple instances here where a guy has shown up with a black eye and we ask and they give you some bull story about tripping down the stairs and yet after it all comes out, eventually you hear that somebody met him out behind the gym or something and "cleaned his clock." (I8-female)

And men, there's a lot more fights and the institution hardly ever hears about half of them because they're taken care of between themselves. I've seen where inmates have shaken down an inmate to make sure there's no weapons and fought, you know, before I can get there. (I35-male)

Women will tell you, make an announcement that they're going to fight ten minutes from now and, therefore, won't fight because everybody has a chance to stop it. But men, if they're gonna fight, they'll just go someplace in the corner and bang, bang, and they come back and have a black eye and they say they fell and hurt his eye and it's over. And they're usually friends after that. (I36-male)

Almost 50 percent of the officers believed women were more assaultive towards each other than male inmates, and an even higher proportion (58 percent) believed that women were more likely to direct aggression towards themselves.

She won't harm anybody else, but she will start to destruct her own body. I've seen them have cuts from here up to their shoulders. They've had stitches in; brand new stitches were put in and they got back here from the hospital and they would sit here and pull the stitches back out again. If you look at their arms, the men don't do it as much as the women, but if you look at the females' arms, they'll sit and they'll just cut and cut and cut. They don't want to hurt anybody else and the only person that they think of hurting is themselves. (I18-female)

Women take it out on themselves. Men will punch a wall if they have to. In fact, a month ago, this inmate, she's assaultive too, but she had taken a plastic knife and cut herself fifteen times across the stomach and then she didn't want to go to the nurse.... So it's more to themselves. (I35-male)

From the officers' responses we get the impression that the aggression of female inmates is emotional, spontaneous, and less physically disabling than the aggression of males, but with fewer rules of acceptable conduct. One suspects that the officers' strong feelings regarding the perceived "viciousness" of female assaults, despite the ironic evidence that more injury occurs during male attacks, has more to do with their distaste for this seemingly unfeminine type of behavior.

Table 4
Responses to the Question: Do Women Inmates Assault Officers More Often Than Men?

	Yes	No
Male Officers	15% (4)	85% (23)[1]
Female Officers	61% (11)	39% (7)

[1] (n=45), x^2 = 10.39, significant at the 0.1 level.

Women's aggression is seen as more frequently directed towards themselves and other female inmates rather than towards officers. The aggression of men is described in very different terms; it is seen as planned, covert, and more often deadly.

There is a possibility that the low percentage of officers who believed women were more assaultive than men could be due to our sample. Male officers were overrepresented (27:18), and it seems logical to assume that female inmates would be less likely to assault male officers. Some support for this assumption was found by disaggregating perceptions of inmate assaultiveness by the sex of the officers as we have done in Table 4. As this table shows, women officers are more likely to perceive women inmates as assaultive.

Some officers, in fact, mentioned this difference in their responses.

... used to be a lot on female c.o.'s, partly because they didn't feel they had to prove themselves with male officers. Women c.o.'s didn't show them respect either, and they would argue with them and let them call them names and call them names back; females know the male c.o.'s wouldn't take it. (I16-male)

Only reason it hasn't happened is lately men are in and the women are acting like glamour dolls for the men, but underneath it all, the women are very assaultive. (I18-female)

The officers, then, expressed the view that women inmates were more likely to assault women officers; that their assaults tend to be spontaneous and uncontrolled, while assaults by males may be more often planned and may stem from a build up of resentments; and while assaults by women may be more frequent, they may less often be serious, perhaps consisting of no more than a shove or push performed in anger.

NOTES

1. K. Burkhart, *Women in Prison* (New York: Popular Library, 1976).

2. R. Ardeti, "The Sexual Segregation of American Prisons," *Yale Law Journal* 82 (1973); 1229–73.

3. R. Toigo, "Illegitimate and Legitimate Cultures in a Training School for Girls," *Proceedings of the Rip Van Winkle Clinic* 13 (Summer 1962); 3–29; A. Lorimer and M. Heads, "The Significance of Morale in a Female Penal Institution," *Federal Probation* 26 (December 1962); 38–44; and I. Moyer, "Prison 'Girls': A Study of Staff Controls of Women in Prison," Paper presented at American Society of Criminology Conference, Washington, D.C., 1981.

4. J. Eyman, *Prisons for Women: A Practical Guide to Administrative Problems* (Springfield, IL.: Charles C. Thomas Publishers, 1971).

5. J. Potter, "In Prison, Women Are Different," *Corrections Magazine* 4 , no. 4 (1978); 17.

6. C. Anderson, "The Female Criminal Offender," *American Journal of Correction* 29 (Nov/Dec, 1967); 7–9; M. Haft, "Women in Prison: Discriminatory Practices and Some Legal Solutions," *Clearinghouse Review* 8 (May 1974); 1–6; General Accounting Office, *Female Offenders: Who Are They and What Are the Problems Confronting Them?* (Washington, D.C.: Government Printing Office, 1979).

7. P. Kissel and J. Seidel, *The Management and Impact of Female Corrections Officers at Jail Facilities Housing Male Inmates* (Boulder, CO: National Institute of Corrections, 1980); J. Potter, "Should Women Guards Work in Prisons for Men?" *Corrections Magazine* 6, no. 5 (1980); 30–38; and L. Zimmer, "Female Guards in Men's Prisons: A Preliminary Report on the Situation in New York and Rhode Island," Unpublished manuscript, 1981.

8. P. Ackerman, "A Staff Group in a Women's Prison," *International Journal of Group Psychotherapy* 22 (July 1972); 364–73.

9. D. Cressey, "Achievement of an Unstated Organizational Goal," in *Prison within Society*, ed. L. Hazelrigg (Garden City, N.Y.: Doubleday, 1968), pp. 50–68.

10. J. Griffith, A. Pennington-Averett and I. Bryan, "Women Prisoners' Multidimensional Locus of Control," *Criminal Justice and Behavior* 8, no. 3 (1981); 386.

11. Moyer, "Prison 'Girls,' " p. 3.

12. M. Zingraff, "Inmate Assimilation: A Comparison of Male and Female Delinquents," *Criminal Justice and Behavior* 7, no. 3 (1980); 275–92.

13. C. Lindquist, "Prison Discipline and the Female Offender," *Journal of Offender Counseling, Services and Rehabilitation* 4, no. 4 (1980); 315.

14. Lindquist, "Prison Discipline," p. 319.

15. D. Street, R. Vinter and C. Perrow, *Organization for Treatment: A Comparative Study of Institutions for Delinquents* (New York: Free Press, 1966).

16. M. Zald, "The Correctional Institution for Juvenile Offenders: An Analysis of Organizational Characters," in *Prison within Society*, pp. 229–47; and "Power Balance and Staff Conflict in Correctional Institutions," in *Prison within Society*, pp. 393–97.

17. D. Cressey, "Contradictory Directives in Complex Organizations: The Case of the Prison," in *Prison within Society*, pp. 477–97.

18. Cressey, "Contradictory Directives," p. 490.

19. Cressey, "Contradictory Directives," p. 491.

20. O. Grusky, "Role Conflict in Organizations: A Study of Prison Camp Officials," in *Prison within Society*, pp. 455–77.

21. These percentages refer to the percentage of officers from the 89 percent who believed women were more emotional than men. Figures do not add up to 100 percent because some officers did not elaborate on what they meant by emotionality.

4

Perceived Supervision Differences and Officer Preferences

When asked if there were differences in the styles of supervision required for men and women inmates, the officers agreed overwhelmingly that different approaches were called for (91 percent). Officers recognized differences in the supervision styles of other officers, and some officers described how they had changed their own supervision style after transferring from a male facility to a female facility or vice versa.

Officers were asked for specific situations in which they might have to treat female inmates and male inmates differently. Seventy-three percent of the officers agreed that there could be situations where they would respond to men and women in different fashions. The situation mentioned most frequently was one in which the officer was required to break up a fight or subdue an inmate. In such a situation, officers, especially male officers, said they would have a tendency to use less force with female inmates. Interestingly, the advice of officers who had experienced such situations was in direct contrast to this preference.

First thing you do is try to separate them. I think that before you use force, maybe voice control might work and then if force is necessary, try to use as little as necessary. But I think that sometimes with the women, voice control will do it. (124-male)

The only thing that I would think would go a little differently is a fight. In an out and out fight, you might use a little less force with the women. (143-female)

Well, if I had an opportunity . . . and I saw two women fighting, I wouldn't
go near them. If I had a water hose, you know, I would use a heavy
duty water hose to separate them . . . because if I approached them
directly, the chances are I was going to get hurt . . . because they don't
know what the hell they're doing when they get that way. . . . I would
be just as scraped up and scratched up and kicked up and punched up
as the opponent and they wouldn't even know they were doing it. . . . I
would be much more prone, if two men were fighting, to get in the
middle, you know, or pull them apart. If I had to break up two women,
I would be much more violent and forceful about it. . . . I think I would
jump in the middle and knock the both of them out right then and
there, or else I know I'm going to get hurt. (P4-male)

I thought I could treat them differently, not be as aggressive and I
almost got hurt myself. Now I've decided that when I see a fight, I'm
going to use as much force as necessary to break it up. (I36-male)

[With men] I would probably walk into a fight and talk to them and
split them up, I mean I wouldn't have to split them up because they
would already be split up probably and I'd have to escort them to special
housing. The men would go, the females would probably fight every
inch of the way. (I39-female)

   Male officers described other differences in supervising women,
such as differences in escort routines, frisk and search procedures,
and the procedures used when taking inmates on outside trips.
   Another situation mentioned was one in which inmates receive
bad news. Officers and counselors alike felt that they have to be
careful in how they break bad news to female inmates and/or be
more empathetic when comforting the female inmates. Officers
and staff seemed to say that males did not ask for counseling or
sympathy from them, and there was almost an element of relief
in the officers' descriptions of the males' stoic reaction to stressful
situations as compared to the emotional release of the females.

If an inmate is upset, I think you tend to take more time with the
females to talk to her. You sort of come out of a mother bag even
though you might be twenty years old. You see, women seem to have
a more mother attitude about it so you would talk to them and find out
what's bothering them where with the men, you might not see the
problem because they keep it to themselves more. (I8-female)

Like with a death in the family, you use more tact and finesse, where with a man, you don't have to go into it because he's not going to let you see much emotion. (I15-female)

I think it's much more difficult to tell a female about a death in the family than it is a male. A male gets, you know he might sit down and cry a little bit, but the females get more hysterical and emotionally involved with it than the male does.... You kind of have to break it to them easier and be more supportive than with the male. The male you can lay it out and say this is what happened, but with the female you have to ... [be] more supportive. (P4-male)

Other interview vignettes suggest that officers felt they had to be more tactful when giving orders to women and that they would have to coax women into completing a task rather than use demands or threats to secure compliance.

With the females, you gotta treat them like you got a lady around all the time. With the males, you know, you're with guys, you say what you want, you do what you want. With the females, you gotta use a little bit of class as far as I'm concerned because they want to be treated that way, and why not? (I27-male)

With men I tell them what I want, with women, I kid them a lot, use some common sense, spend more time trying to supervise them. With men, orders are immediate. (I16-male)

You have to be more motherly with the female inmates as opposed to a male institution because the male inmates can be told what to do in a more direct way and they'll do it. But if you be direct with a female, she will give you less response and you have to be very much more specific and tactful with a female inmate when you give female inmates instructions or orders. You just can't be as forceful with a female because they're not going to respond to that. There are different ways to get them to do something ... very tactful, tender loving care, call them pet names, and for God's sake, don't be too direct. (I36-male)

All of these supervision differences are consistent with the inmate differences we discussed in the previous chapter. It seems clear that at least in some cases, officer perceptions, i.e., women's greater emotionality, are linked to real changes in officer performance.

PERCEIVED GENDER DIFFERENCES IN SUPERVISION

One interesting component of interview results was the officers' perceptions of differences in supervision patterns of men and women and difficulties of cross-sex supervision. It became apparent from officers' descriptions of supervision methods that men and women performed the correctional officer role somewhat differently. Both males and females described differences in supervision style by sex of the officer in addition to sex of the inmate. Since male officers were more likely to have had their training in maximum security prisons with more rigid rules of conduct and less interaction with inmates, they sensed an absence of a strong officer subculture and "united front" against the inmates when they were exposed to female facilities. Because of greater communication with inmates, officers do not develop the camaraderie which is remembered with fondness by those who worked in maximum security prisons for men.

In the male facilities, I think the officers know that they depend on each other a lot, they know that you need Officer Jones or Officer Jackson or whoever if there is a problem; here, I don't know. Women— it's a lot different. . . . They've never been in a real maximum so they don't realize, they don't understand the seriousness of it all. You have some who have worked in the male facilities and you can tell the difference. (I23-male)

There is also some doubt about the ability of female officers to perform in a crisis.

Most women like the men to be here 'cause they know if there's trouble, the men are going to react. The man is gonna react, either way, he's gonna come in and help. (I18-female)

The women, the woman correctional officer and the women inmates, they tend to back up. I'm not putting them down, most of the women correctional officers are good, but they cannot handle themselves in a male institution. They're not assertive enough. (I35-male)

Well, the officers in BH, I find they didn't respond very well. . . . When . . . a female acted up we tried to reason with her, we gave her a reasonable length of time to settle down ... but if she wouldn't move, then we'd get a small group ... to pick her up and move her. And in BH, they'll talk to her for like an hour or so and didn't assert themselves. (P1-female)

Female officers, on the other hand, see male officers as possibly too vulnerable to the manipulative blandishments of female inmates. A perceived tendency by male officers to employ "old guard" methods of supervision also caused perceived conflicts. Even when female officers do not specifically object to male methods of control, they described incongruities which occurred when a "hard nosed" supervision style coexists with a style more empathetic to inmates' needs.

You take a man's prison, men tend to be "old guard" and seem to be more punitive. My feeling is they talk about the old ways, going back to the old system when everybody lines up and walks in a line and spoke when spoken to. You know, old guard. And it's very difficult to change old guard to the new ideas in corrections. Old guards saw their ways work.... I find that females tend to relate to the inmates with more respect. Women seem to be able to be more ... empathetic. (I3-female)

I know I have seen the male officers laugh at us and say, "why do you explain this to them, you don't have to explain nothing to these inmates, you just tell them yes or no." Women are a little more soft, I think, in that area, because we feel that we like to be treated decent and so we try to treat other people decent.... Now whether that's the right approach or not, I don't know. It's worked for me and I'm not about to change it. With the men, they are more, they're very short and curt with their answers to the inmates quite often and yet they can get away with it. The male officers feel they are not counselors, that there are paid counselors here to tend to the inmates' problems. And quite often your women don't feel that way because we know that at nighttime there is no counselor on duty as a rule and if somebody's upset at 8:00 tonight, you don't tell them to wait until tomorrow morning to see a counselor if you feel you can talk to them. At least get a little insight into what's bothering them, you know. It could prevent a problem later on, or if the inmate does something a little weird later on, at least you'll understand why and so will the powers that be when you finish writing a report. (I8-female)

It is alleged by both male and female officers that female officers are somewhat more likely to be receptive to the problems of inmates and that they even try to draw them out at times.

Usually when you work with these inmates day after day, you can tell when they're upset. You see a change in their attitude or they're just not acting like themselves, and you go up to them and say, "What's wrong?" and nine times out of ten they'll open up to you. They might not tell you the entire truth, or if it's something they really don't want you to know, they'll tell you a little bit and say "I'd rather not talk about it." Whether they would with a male officer, I don't know. (I8-female)

There was a different relationship between the male officer and the inmates. It's changed a lot, but when I first came in, the male officers, especially those who came from maximum securities, at the camp they spoke when they were spoken to, but they didn't go out of their way to accost the inmate. Where the women, I found, if they saw a guy looking kind of down, would say, "You got a problem?" (I15-female)

I would suspect that the female officers, because they're put in that mother role, probably tend to let the inmates get away with a little more than the male officers do. The male officers have to be ... very professional in the way in which they carry out their duties. For example, a female officer could get away with calling somebody "honey," a male officer could not. ... So the two officers try to carry themselves very differently out of necessity. Some female officers are very authoritarian, carry themselves very formally. Most of them can relax a little bit. They can touch somebody, they can put their arm around a shoulder, and they do. (P8-female)

Critics of the empathetic style of supervision sometimes point out that familiarity—as they see it—can contribute to a breach of security, and compromise necessary social distance between officers and inmates.

The inmate should be taught that an officer is there as a person they can learn from and that they should respect and deal with, but a lot of the staff can't handle that and they make friends with the inmates and they hope that the inmates will follow the rules because of the friendship that has developed. And that's one reason why we do have our problems from time to time, because it doesn't work. It happens with male officers too, but on different levels. The female officers are in constant conflict with the female inmates because they deal with them as peers and I've heard inmates and female officers arguing over hairdos to a point where it almost becomes an argument, and makeup and things of this nature, which is not professional. And the female officers, in my personal opinion, did not develop the degree of professionalism needed to work with prisoners and not get themselves involved in the issues that they do get themselves involved in. (I19-male)

I think people ... tend to forget who's in charge. ... They forget it and the officer has to regain the control, and sometimes the officer has to come down a little quicker, a little harsher. (P7-male)

In a male institution, you can have a relationship with an inmate and still when push comes to shove, it's understood with the officer and the inmate, they're an inmate and you're an officer and they understand you have to do what you have to do and they have to do what they have to do. Where here it seems like if you have a relationship with an inmate, it seems like they feel betrayed when you have to do things like an officer. They feel betrayed, they have a tendency to want to be a friend and not realize that you're an officer. (I25-male)

Relationships with Inmates

When we describe officers' relationships with inmates, we are concerned with four types of interactions: male officers with male inmates; male officers with female inmates; female officers with female inmates; and female officers with male inmates. There are similarities in the relationship of an officer of either sex and a male inmate; likewise, there are similarities between the relationship of an officer of either sex and a female inmate. However, the interaction between officers and the inmates of the opposite sex was the most frequent topic of discussion in the interviews.

Both males and female officers tend to find male inmates easier to work with, but this difference emerged more sharply among women officers. Female officers, more so than male officers, tend to find that male inmates respond to them with respect and are willing to follow orders. In contrast, while the majority of male officers did not express a preference for working with women, they did report less trouble than women officers in supervising

them. While 83 percent of female officers reported women inmates as more difficult to supervise, only 55 percent of male
correctional officers believed this to be true.

I don't think any woman, no matter how bad she is, wants to look bad
in the eyes of the opposite sex. (I2-female)

The women have a tendency to befriend a male officer easily. 'Cause
guys, I suppose, will be guys more or less, and the same thing goes for
women, you know. (I7-male)

If the female inmates like the male officers, they will go out of their
way to do things for him. (I18-female)

Female officers also described advantages to dealing with the
opposite sex.

I think the men are far more respectful. Maybe it's because they're
dealing with a woman, and you know, they feel they have to, but I
never hear them swearing. (I4-female)

I've had nowhere near the same problems with men as I've had with
the women. Being the same sex seems to make a difference. At least I
have found and some of the other female officers, the men here tend
to give you much more respect. They respect the male officer too, but
in a different way. They will talk back to a male officer much quicker
than they will the female officer, at least I have found that. And the
same applies with the women. The women will be far more mouthy
with the female officer than they will with the male officer. (I8-female)

Being a female they try to please you because you're an officer and
because you're a female. To look good in front of you like a gentleman
or whatever. Sometimes I talk to them nice and they do more things
for you. (I7-female)

I've only had maybe two or three instances where they come out in a
towel and I've told them that's out, you know....The majority ...do
come out dressed....When a male inmate curses and there's a female
around, nine times out of ten they'll apologize and they'll try to hold
back. I know when there's two males on the unit, two male officers, I'm
sure they curse a lot more, but if they do slip, they always seem to

apologize and ... if someone doesn't ... someone will say, "Hey, watch your mouth, watch what you're saying." (I41-female)

A woman don't care whether a woman likes them or not. You know, they don't care. I'm here and I'm going to do what I'm gonna do and you can't tell me what to do, you're just a woman like I am. But then when they have a problem, the tune is different. The women don't care if women like them, men do care. (I42-male)

The lousiest male inmate ... has this much respect for a female, they all had a mother, o.k.? There are a few exceptions, your bugs, your mentally deranged people, people with really warped minds. But I'm talking the male population as a whole has got 2 percent respect for any woman as long as you treat them like a man and respect them as a person, o.k.? That's not true for a female. A female has a mother, yes, but that, I think is one reason why males can relate better to the women than I can and I can relate better to the males than they can. I think it's the difference of opposites. Your female is basically oriented towards the female figure. So my feeling, overall, is that if you treat these people with, you know, a little bit of respect and as another human being ... then you will always get a certain amount of respect back, with a few exceptions. Plus, there's a certain fear factor that's instilled in a male facility with females working in it, o.k.? It's not ever said point blank, but those male inmates know that if they ever touch a female officer, you'd have the course and you can't say the same thing to females. (I43-female)

The relationship between male officers and male inmates is perceived as formal, with almost businesslike communication patterns and very little personal interaction. Exceptions are seen only in cases where there has been long and stable contact between the officer and inmate, and then usually only in terms of superficial "baseball game" conversations.

I find that when I worked in a male facility, I get along better with the men. The men realize that they're there to do their time, and I'm there to do a job, and as long as we both realize this, we get along very well together. (I34-male)

In a male institution, everything is everyday. It's always the same, the men, they have their jobs, they're looking forward to going to work, going to their assignments. They might not agree with the rules, but they'll follow them. They might not like you, but you don't work as a friend or a big brother or a mother. To them you're like a boss, a foreman on the job. You're not in love with your foreman, but they'll follow the rules. (I37-male)

I think in my dealing with female inmates, it's more like a father type image and when dealing with male inmates it's more a police type image—an authoritarian figure. (I10-male)

Relationships between female officers and female inmates were seen, if anything, as too emotional, according to several officers. The perception is that the personal communication patterns which seem to occur more frequently with female inmates may oftentimes lead to overfamiliarity which sometimes has disrupting consequences. Although this danger is perceived to hold especially for female officers, there was a parallel concern about male officers getting too involved with female inmates during daily supervision. Several interviewees remarked that males change their supervision styles in this regard when they get transferred to a facility housing women inmates.

I just think that a male ... goes there and he decides that, you know, they sent me here to straighten this out and to help out or something in shaping this place up. They go in there with that perception, I think, and the next thing you know they're talking about the "girls" and ... I'll say something like "Jeez, she stabbed somebody. You give somebody 30 days for stabbing somebody? You wouldn't do that in a male facility." ... To me, they change because they're there. (P7-male)

This supervision style is one which is more "lenient" in the sense of explaining rules and spending more time listening to problems. Several officers made analogies between their supervision style with women and a mother or father role.

Here you're more like a mother or father image and they look at you like that because somebody's always hadda tell 'em here. With females you always gotta tell them what to do. With the males, just explain to them what you want done and they'll do it. The females are always hanging around correction officers. With the males, they would rather be with themselves than hanging around a correction officer, here that's all they do. (I37-male)

We became part of their family; really, some of them we were the only family they ever had. (P1-female)

I think the staff, some of the staff, get a lot more involved in the personal problems of the inmates than they do in the male facilities. Partially because the women are more apt to some staff to open up personally, and the males don't open up personally. I think that's the major difference, is the personal type relationships that are in here. (P12-male)

If these perceptions are true, it is interesting, then, to ponder the question, are women officers more empathetic because they deal with women inmates; or are women inmates more open because they have a sympathic ear with female officers. There is obviously an interaction between "female" characteristics and "male" characteristics of both inmates and officers. The most affectional, sympathetic relationship is between female officers and female inmates, but this can lead to problems of overfamiliarity. On the other end of the spectrum, the male officer–male inmate relationship is characterized as cold, rational, and businesslike. There are no problems remembering one's role, but neither is there much warmth or empathy. Which type of work environment do most officers prefer?

OFFICER PREFERENCES

It probably comes as no surprise that officers were more likely to prefer working with men than women. Sixty-eight percent of the officers said they preferred supervising male inmates, and 67 percent agreed that female inmates were harder to supervise. Although the description of this difference held for both male and female officers, female officers were more likely to prefer working with males and were more likely to feel that female inmates were harder to supervise. The proportion of officer responses, broken down by sex, are presented in Table 5.

Basically the preferences of officers can be depicted by the four-group classification as presented in Table 6.

Among officers who preferred working with male inmates and who also believed that women inmates were harder to supervise (Category B: 53 percent), there were differences in the reasons

Table 5
Officer Responses to the Question: Do You Prefer Working With Male Inmates or Female Inmates?[1]

	Prefer Working With:		
	Male Inmates	Female Inmates	No Preference
Male Officers	66% (18)	11% (3)	22% (6)
Female Officers	72% (13)	11% (2)	16% (3)

Are female inmates more difficult than male inmates to supervise?[2]

	Yes	No
Male Officers	55% (15)	44% (12)
Female Officers	83% (15)	16% (3)

[1](N=45); A significance test was inappropriate due to the small numbers in some of the cells.

[2](N=45); A chi-square test was performed and it showed there was a significant interaction between the sex of the two officers and the responses (.05 level).

Table 6
Correctional Officers' Supervision Preferences

	Prefer to Supervise	
Believe women are more difficult to supervise	Women	Men
	(A) prefer women even though they are more difficult (27%)	(B) prefer men because women are more difficult (53%)
	(C) prefer women because they are not more difficult (4%)	(D) prefer men even though women are not more difficult (16%)

given for the relative difficulty by male officers and female officers. Male officers were more likely to mention difficulties caused by being custodians of the opposite sex. A major concern seemed to be the possibility of being framed for rape by an inmate. This sentiment was exacerbated by the belief that female superiors and administrators might not support the officers in such a situation.

Other reasons given by the male officers for their belief that female inmates were harder to deal with were tied to perceived differences in how they needed to behave towards the women. The officers felt they had to be careful with their speech in front of female inmates. They also felt that with women, they would be more inhibited in situations that required the exercise of force.

I know how to handle men. Now with a female, all my life I've been brought up to protect them and respect them so when you have to use force, it's difficult. (I16-male)

I can deal with the males if I have to. If a fight is necessary between an officer and an inmate, I can deal better with the male because he's a male. With the female, the supervisors don't like a male officer beating up on a female. We've had several incidents where a female has struck a male officer and the male officer has not struck back, but the first question out of the supervisor's mouth is whether the male has touched the inmate. (I29-male)

I don't think I dealt with women long enough ... to get away from being ... very sympathetic to them. (P6-male)

I think males relate to women being girlfriends, wives, mothers. . . . Women are about to kill you and you're careful about how you're touching her. . . . The perception is different, you know, the man has to get used to dealing with the women as ... an inmate. He has to see them in that role rather than looking at them as a female. (P6-male)

Ironically, perceived sex differences were also important to those female officers who preferred working with males. Male inmates were seen as more likely than female inmates to treat women officers with respect. There was also a feeling among female officers that the male inmates appreciated them as women, and this feeling was reported as making their job more enjoyable. Both male and female officers mentioned other reasons why they generally preferred working with males. Most of these reasons related to the demands and complaints officers expected from women and/or their refusal to follow orders.

Women tend to show their problems more. Things bother them more so they have to act out more than the men. So that part there makes it a little harder, because you have more problems to deal with. I know I spent eight hours with the men the other night ... and ... nobody bothered you. They all stayed in their rooms like they were supposed to.... But now if I was over with the women ... I'm sure there would be some women wandering around and bugging you.... Some stupid things, like some of them will wait for the middle of the night to ask you for an address to write the Commissioner, whatever pops in their minds at the time that seems important to them. (I8-female)

I'd much rather supervise men. The men will take an order, they will respond to an order. If there's any question of the order, it will be resolved through dialogue; it will very seldom become violent. Females are contrary to that. If they don't like what they hear, they will provoke violence by means of profanity, overt acts on their part. And if a person isn't really on their guard, they could react. They will bring a strong person down to a breaking point, and I've seen it done. It takes a lot of years of maturity in the system to work with females. Not that I'm trying to credit myself, but I feel that only because of my years am I able to deal with them. (I19-male)

They had to know, why? How come? They would be more apt to question what I said. Whether they knew I was right or wrong. They would have to question it just for the sake of questioning it. (I2-female)

There was only a small number of officers (in Categories C: 4 percent and D: 16 percent) who did not believe women were harder to supervise. These officers felt that women did not pose more difficult, but only different, supervision problems from those with men. The reasons these officers gave for preferring to supervise some inmates rather than others varied. For instance, several male officers held the view that officers should only supervise inmates of the same sex. Others expressed the view that female inmates were more enjoyable to be around.

You can enjoy the women even though they're convicted criminals.... Women do like to enjoy their life, even if they are in jail, they still have a sense of humor ... and they keep things sort of lighthearted in the prison system. (I8-female)

I like the women better because it's a learning experience. Talking about cooking and such together with the women is enjoyable. (I40-female)

A few officers preferred the women because they felt safer supervising women. This was true especially for male officers.

You got the tendency to get reckless. You can get away with more things than with a guy. It's easier to keep them in check and, plus, maybe because I'm such a big guy, if something does happen, you can always pull women apart. (I7-male)

The most interesting group were those officers (in Category A: 27 percent) who agreed that women were more difficult to supervise, but still preferred to work with them. Basically, these individuals enjoyed the challenge of trying to meet women's demands and solving women's problems. They also enjoyed the variety, unpredictability, and constant turmoil that was likely to be present in settings for women.

Men are less stressful to work with, but you get bored with them.... You keep active with the women so I enjoy that more. They have more problems you have to deal with. (I28-female)

I find it a lot more challenging because they are so demanding and because they appear to care a lot more about what's happening to them while they're incarcerated. I found the men boring to work with. Minimal problems and minimal hassles and they just wanted to do time and most of them were able to do that, and it was very dull. There was no challenge to that, although it was easier, less stressful. (P8-female)

It seems that, along with the desire to avoid boredom, the staff who preferred working with women were more interested in getting seriously involved in rehabilitation, even though that involvement might be stressful and carried the risk that the officers might be manipulated by the inmates.

I prefer women because you feel like you accomplish more, you could get to them better.... The ones that act out are the ones that change, it's more satisfying. (I14-female)

I think the majority of people would prefer to work with men just because it's so much less stressful.... Staff has to be careful not to get over involved. Women are so much more open and sharing about what's going on inside their hearts than men are. Sometimes it's just another manipulation technique that's used to engender sympathy, pity, whatever ... but because people are human, and anytime someone opens up to you, allowing you to experience what she's experiencing, the tendency is you start to care about that individual, which is also a lot more stressful. (P8-female)

When they had problems, they came; whereas the men didn't.... They have a problem, they wear it on their sleeve. They'd come down and talk to you about it all the time and they were just more open, more fun.... Men were a lot easier to work with.... If you were interested in control, men were a lot easier to work with. I think if you were interested in the security of the facility ... if you were interested in the order and procedure ... everything except treatment, I would prefer the men. It's an easier "bit" so to speak.... If you want to come to a facility and not know what the day is going to bring ... if you enjoy that type of excitement, women every time. (P5-male)

5

The Perceptions of Co-Correctional Officers

The introduction of co-correctional facilities has provided researchers with an excellent opportunity to study the prison behavior of men and women in the same facility. This is important for a number of reasons. First, attempts to compare men's and women's behavior as measured, for instance, by disciplinary tickets, are beset by problems when one tries to use records from two different facilities; there are inevitable differences in reporting procedures; what may be considered serious enough to report in one facility may be ignored in the other. Another problem is that institutional differences may influence the different behavior patterns manifested by the inmates. One institution may be treatment-oriented while the other institution may be custody-oriented. Size, location of the facility, and the demographics of the staff all may affect inmate behavior. A certain amount of the variance measured would thus not be caused by the sex of the inmates, but rather by one or more of the above factors.

When men and women are housed in the same facility, these problems are somewhat alleviated, although there are still problems in comparability, i.e., disproportional sex ratios, differences in average ages or offense histories, unequal program opportunities, and sex-specific restrictions on inmate movement. These remaining problems, of course, necessitate continued caution in interpreting findings of behavior differences between the sexes or, in our case, of perceived differences.

Among officers interviewed for this study, fourteen had experience in a co-correctional facility. Because this setting is, in many ways, different from a single-sex facility, the officers' perceptions might be expected to be different from those who have only worked in single-sex institutions.

As some writers remind us, co-corrections is actually a step into the past. It was not until 1873 that the first prison for women was built. Before that time, penal institutions housed both men and women, first, in the same large common rooms; then, later, in separate wings or areas of the facility.[1] In the 1970s, the idea of co-corrections was rediscovered, and in 1971, the Federal Youth Center in Morgantown began housing both males and females, followed by the Federal Correctional Institution at Ft. Worth. The first state facility for both sexes was opened in Framingham, Massachusetts, in 1973. In close succession, other federal facilities and a number of state facilities adopted a co-correctional format, so that by 1980, 58 percent of the women and 7.5 percent of the men who were incarcerated in federal institutions were housed in a co-correctional facility, and 9.7 percent of the states' incarcerated women and 0.53 percent of the incarcerated men were in co-correctional facilities.[2]

A number of evaluation studies are now available on co-correctional facilities. These studies have examined the expectations, goals, and success in meeting stated goals of the co-correctional facilities now in operation. Ross cites some of the reasons why facilities were changed to house both sexes. Among the reasons he cites are reduction of the dehumanizing effects of confinement by allowing heterosexual relationships; reduction of institutional control problems by weakening disruptive homosexual activity, lessening of assaultive behavior; protection for weaker inmates in a predominantly same-sex institution; creation of a more normal, less institutional atmosphere; realization of economies of scale in terms of more efficient utilization of available space, staff, and programs; relief of immediate or anticipated overcrowding; reduction in need for civilian labor, by provision of both light and heavy work forces; program offerings and equal access for males and females; expansion of treatment potentials for working with inmates having "sexual problems" and development of positive heterosexual relationships and coping skills; relief of immediate or anticipated legal pressure to provide equal access to programs and services to both sexes; and expanded career opportunities for women previously "boxed into" single state women's institutions as correctional staff.[3] We see that the stated goals incorporate both control and treatment orientations but the treatment goals have probably been the more publicized.

Evaluation studies have uncovered some adverse effects of housing men and women together. The first disadvantage affects both officers and inmates. The perceived need to keep the sexes apart adds to the officers' work load and further restricts inmates' freedom to move within facility grounds. As Ross points out, women are disproportionately the objects of this control because of possible pregnancies. Women may also be relegated to or choose to play passive dependency roles with the arrival of males, as opposed to the fuller range of opportunities in single-sex institutions.[4] Access to programs for one sex or another may also be reduced if officer supervision is deemed necessary. Finally, it is possible that family relationships may suffer due to the incarcerated spouses' close proximity to members of the opposite sex.

We are primarily interested in the expectation that co-corrections can reduce institutional control problems. Evaluations generally find that housing men and women together reduces the incidence of homosexuality and assaults, at least for males. These studies have also shown that in co-correctional facilities, program participation increases, self-image measures show improvement, and social skills are enhanced through interaction with the opposite sex.[5]

As noted, a major problem in co-corrections seems to be the difficulty of preventing sexual involvements and pregnancies, which, as one writer points out, is primarily a problem because of public and staff disapproval of inmate sexual activities. Heterosexuality poses control problems in the same way that homosexual liaisons do in single-sex institutions. Such problems include not only the regulation of sexual liaisons, but the fights that evolve out of love triangles and jealousy. Although discipline "tags" for assaults are lower in co-correctional facilities, the overall number of all infractions is higher due to rule violations of regulations governing interaction between the sexes.[6] Officer frustration develops because the officers are pressured to prevent these inmate sexual involvements.[7]

A few studies have taken advantage of the opportunity to study behavioral differences between the sexes in co-correctional facilities. One dealt with participation in programs, and concluded that co-corrections interferes with the males' opportunities for rehabilitation. In this study women were described as less mature, less responsible, and more dependent than males. According to the author, behavior of the women due to these personality traits disrupted programs, classrooms, and the institution as a whole, thus endangering educational opportunities for males. Women in the facility were also reported to have lower IQ's than the men, which resulted in a retardation of the educational process.[8]

According to another study, women received more disciplinary "tags" than the men did in the same facility (0.143 tickets for men as compared to 0.446 for women, per month).[9] More women than men were involved in academic programs (66.7% versus 57.71%); however, a larger percentage of men than women claimed the goal of a college degree (21.2% versus 1.3%). Equal numbers of men and women desired or were involved in vocational programs; however, there were differences in the types of programs men and women aspired to. As might be expected, these differences were influenced by sex stereotypes, and women disproportionately sought cosmetology or sewing programs, while the men more often requested meat cutting, welding, or office machine repair classes. There were similar differences in long-range goals. Women, more often than men, mentioned family or personal relationships among their goals, and while both men and women mentioned jobs, men were more likely to anticipate owning their own businesses. Wilson noted that in her sample, women were more likely to request counseling, but she cautioned that this finding was probably a function of a sampling method which eliminated "extreme" groups of men, such as addicts or the elderly, who were housed in separate living units.[10]

The other finding which can be gleaned from the literature is that correctional staff treat men and women differently within the same institution. We have already mentioned the claim that women are more frequently the object of rule enforcement in the administration's efforts to keep the sexes apart. It has also been noted, however, that punitive transfer is a more frequently exercised option when sanctioning males, due to the greater number of available facilities. For the same offense, a male inmate may thus be transferred while the female inmate is allowed to stay in the co-correctional facility.

Another study found that for similar offenses women tended to receive more lenient sentences.[11] Relative leniency has been cited as harmful to female offenders because it tolerates, and thus reinforces, their immature behavior.

The greater immaturity of the women and the staff's willingness to tolerate it results in disruption of prison routines and inequitable administration of discipline . . . large numbers of women are late for work or school or go to sick call to avoid doing their jobs. Rather than altering the women's behavior through firm discipline, the staff seems to positively reinforce their immaturity. Many times women will leave classes early, disrupting the class with their exit and the rest of the institution with their wandering around in unexpected places. As a general rule, women receive less punishment for the same offenses than do men. Moreover, the staff tolerates profanity from the women, but not from the men. Accepting such childish behavior insures that prisoners will continue to act childishly. . . . Although women are watched more closely than the men, probably because there are only 100 women to 400 men, they receive privileges and preferential treatment from the staff under the same sort of double standard applied in disciplinary matters. For example, it is much easier for a women to see the warden or an associate warden.[12]

CORRECTIONAL OFFICER PERCEPTIONS

Unfortunately, we do not have a large number of correctional officers with co-correctional facility experience in our sample whose responses we can analyze. Table 7 compares select responses of co-correctional officers to those of other officers.

Significantly fewer co-correctional officers (than officers who have not worked in a co-correctional facility) believed women to

Table 7

Perceptions of Inmate Sex Differences by Officers with Different Work Experiences (Select Items)

RESPONSES

	YES		NO	
	Co-Corr. Officers	Single-Sex Officers	Co-Corr. Officers	Single-Sex Officers
Perceived Personality Differences:				
*Are women more emotional than men?	71% (10)	96% (30)	29% (4)	4% (1)
Are women more demanding than men?	92% (13)	86% (25)	8% (1)	14% (6)
Are women more complaining than men?	64% (9)	74% (23)	36% (5)	26% (8)
Are women more manipulative than men?[1]	71% (10)	54% (17)	29% (4)	46% (14)
Perceived Behavior Differences:				
*Are women more assaultive toward inmates than men?	22% (3)	61% (19)	88% (11)	39% (12)
Are women more assaultive toward officers than men?	15% (2)	42% (13)	85% (12)	58% (18)
Do women "act out" more than men?	71% (10)	90% (28)	39% (4)	10% (3)
*Do women refuse to follow orders more than men?	43% (6)	88% (24)	57% (8)	22% (7)
*Do women cause more problems for officers due to their homosexual behavior?[1]	36% (5)	71% (22)	64% (9)	29% (9)
Perceived Supervision Differences:				
Are there differences in supervising men and women?	78% (11)	96% (30)	22% (3)	4% (1)

*Fisher's Exact Test was performed. Those items marked by an asterisk reached significance levels of .05 or better.

Table 7 (*continued*)

	RESPONSES			
	YES		NO	
	Co-Corr. Officers	Single-Sex Officers	Co-Corr. Officers	Single-Sex Officers
Are women harder to supervise?	50% (7)	74% (23)	50% (7)	26% (8)
Do you prefer to supervise?				
Women.........	8% (1)	12% (4)		
Men..........	78% (11)	66% (20)		
No preference.	15% (2)	22% (7)		

be more emotional and/or assaultive towards other inmates. Fewer also believed women were more prone to "acting out" behaviors or refusing orders. Interestingly, co-correctional officers were more likely than officers in single-sex facilities to perceive women as more childish than men.

In terms of supervision differences, co-correctional officers may be likely to perceive differences in problems of supervision, and less likely to believe there are situations where different treatment is necessary, although these differences did not reach the .05 significance level. Paradoxically, co-correctional officers may be more likely than single-sex officers to prefer working with men than with women, and less likely than officers in single-sex institutions to have no preference in the type of inmate they prefer to supervise. These differences in perceptions are unlikely to be due to a difference in the proportions of male and female officers, since 57 percent of the officers of the co-correctional sample were male and 61 percent of the single-sex institution sample were male.

The interview findings lend support to the hypothesis that co-correctional institutions may have a moderating effect on women's behavior. According to officers with co-correctional experience, females are less assaultive and less prone to produce problems related to homosexual activity. Officers explain these behavior differences in terms of the inmates' fear of transfer (inmates enjoy the privacy, freedom, and greater safety of the co-correctional facility). Another reason cited is that there is a definite influence on inmate behavior by the presence of the opposite sex.

Officers describe women inmates as attempting to attract and maintain male boyfriends in prison much as they would on the outside. Several officers jokingly referred to their "fence program," which was a term used to describe the relationships which developed through the fence that separated the respective recreation yards of the men and women inmates.

Being a co-ed place, women tend to act more like ladies here because they have their male friend on the other side of the fence who says, "I don't want to hear you talk like that." You see, they like to be bossed around by men, most women do, even though they talk about ERA and everything, they still have that. Well, you know, this has been the way society has been for many centuries and, uh, as much as they holler about equal rights, they like a man to say, "Look, you're my woman and I don't want to hear any crap out of your mouth. When I tell you to come, you come, if I don't want you by the fence, don't you come near the fence." And they won't. It's amazing how they obey. . . . They like feeling that they belonged to somebody and this man was going to take care of them, and of course, they made all their big fantasy plans too. It was amazing to watch how they liked to be dominated, even though there was a fence separating them. I used to kid them and tell them to tell him to "sit on it—you don't have to take that" and they'd say, "Oh, he'll kill me" and they really believed that somehow he'd get after them for not obeying. The other funny thing was that they talk constantly about "nobody bosses me around," and then five minutes later they've got a man on the other side of the fence bossing them around and they love it. It keeps them in line. If this was all female you would have more grief and aggravation, you know, the screaming and the fights. And there would probably be more homosexuality here. You find very little, because even though maybe every girl in C building doesn't go to that fence, but the majority of them do and they stand there and they talk and they make plans for getting out and then probably never see each other again. But it's something to do every day. And they write little love notes, which they're not supposed to. It gives them something to do every day. They can't wait till the yard opens. Plus, I find that they take much better care of themselves physically.

They will dress. They won't go outside the building unless they've got makeup on and they look very nice. Where you don't find that as much when you're in an all female facility, where they're not really trying to impress anybody. (18-female)

Officers did not see themselves supervising men and women in a discriminatory manner, though a few did believe that women had more rules to follow, and that more restrictions were placed on their movements. This was, in fact, true, given the system of control which had been set up to prevent illicit contact between the sexes.

The findings are suggestive, though they must be interpreted with caution due to the small numbers involved. From this information we may hypothesize that there is a moderation in the extreme behavior differences of men and women in co-correctional facilities, that co-correctional facilities decrease the amount of homosexuality and assaultiveness among both men and women, and that there is less of a tendency to supervise the sexes differently in the same facility than when they are housed in separate facilities.

NOTES

1. B. Ruback, "The Sexually Integrated Prison—A Legal and Policy Evaluation," *American Journal of Criminal Law* 3 (1975); 310–30.

2. J. G. Ross, *Studying the Coed Joint—A Case Study in the NEP Process for Synthesizing Evaluations and Assessing Evaluability* (Washington, D.C.: NCJRS, 1978); and J. G. Ross, E. Heffernan, J. Sevick and F. Johnson, *National Evaluation Program, Phase I Report Assessment of Co-educational Corrections* (Washington, D.C.: National Institute of Law Enforcement and Criminal Justice, 1978).

3. J. G. Ross, *Studying the Coed Joint*, p. 15.

4. J. G. Ross, *Studying the Coed Joint*, p. 10; also see C. Schweber, "Beauty Marks and Blemishes: The Coed Prison as a Microcosm of Integrated Society," *Prison Journal* 64, no. 1 (1985); 3–15; J. Smykla, "A Phenomenological Analysis of the Social Environment in a Coed Prison," Dissertation, Michigan State University, 1978; and, J. Smykla, *Co-Corrections: A Case Study of a Coed Federal Prison* (Washington, D.C.: University Press of America, 1978).

5. D. Anderson, "Co-Corrections," *Corrections Magazine* 4, no. 3

(1978); 32–41; J. Mablis, et al., "Co-Corrections Evaluation—Preliminary Data," *Offender Rehabilitation* 2 no. 4 (1978); 303–325.

6. Mablis, "Co-Corrections Evaluation," p. 310.

7. Anderson, "Co-Corrections," p. 41.

8. Ruback, "The Sexually Integrated Prison," p. 326.

9. N. K. Wilson, "Styles of Doing Time in a Coed Prison," in *Co-Corrections*, ed. J. Smykla (New York: Human Services Press, 1980), p. 161.

10. N. K. Wilson, "Styles of Doing Time in a Coed Prison," p. 165.

11. Anderson, "Co-Corrections," p. 38.

12. Ruback, "The Sexually Integrated Prison," p. 321.

6

Explaining the Differences and Implications for Management

So far we have described perceived differences in the behavior of male and female inmates and have shown that most officers feel women are more difficult to supervise. This chapter concerns the officers' explanations of these differences. Attribution theory provides a framework for understanding officers' explanations of their perceptions; it explores "naive psychology" or common sense. It is a taxonomy of how people deal with available information to arrive at inferences about causation. The importance of personal attributions in social psychology is that they illuminate a person's reaction to others and his or her behavior in a social situation. By being able to understand the thought processes that make up a person's understanding of a social event or another person's behavior, one can more easily predict how the interpreter will react in any given situation.

Heider sets forth three assumptions fundamental to attribution theory. The first holds that an adequate understanding of a person's behavior is contingent on the description of how this person perceives and describes his social world. The second assumption is that people desire to predict and control their environment, and that prediction is possible only if people are able to interpret and infer the causal antecedents of behavior. Heider's third assumption is that there are some basic similarities between object and person perception. Predictability in the social world is achieved by the same processes that are involved in the perception of the physical world.[1]

Theorists have identified some basic elements in the process of assigning causation. It seems that individuals use the same steps as those involved in scientific inquiry, such as the covariation principle, "an effect is attributed to one of its possible causes with which, over time, it co-varies."[2] The process of selecting the factor or combination of factors that one assumes has caused a certain event or behavior involves reliance on the criteria of "distinctiveness," "consensus," and "consistency." In other words, a person knows that his response is an accurate or valid one if (a) the response is distinctively associated with the stimulus; (b) the response is similar to those made by other persons to the same stimulus (consensus); and (c) the response is consistent over time or in successive exposures to the stimulus over different sensory and perceptual modalities.[3]

A choice any interpreter of behavior has to make in resolving issues of causation is whether the behavior is caused by characteristics of the person or by characteristics of the situation. It has been discovered that while individuals are more likely to use a situational explanation to explain their own behavior, an observer is more likely to use person attribution to explain any other actor's behavior. In other words, we tend to explain the behavior of another person by pointing to qualities of the other person, i.e., by assuming that they always act like that. One is also more likely to use person attribution if no information supports multiple causation.[4]

In our study, officers could have attributed the behavior differences of men and women to the situation, to the individual, or to qualities of the groups themselves. We asked the officers for their "explanations" of the perceived differences to determine whether they favored a person or situation attribution. Before these findings are presented, it is useful to review the concepts of distinctiveness, consensus, and consistency from the perspective of the officers.

Distinctiveness refers to a situation wherein the behavior at issue can be uniquely associated with the person or group. We have been concerned with a number of behaviors which are attributed to women in prison more frequently than to men. They are not viewed as discrete behavior patterns of the sexes; that is, no officer ventured to say that males never acted emotionally or females never hid their emotions. The attribution is, therefore, always context-related. But, in general, officers were willing and felt able to attach specific behavior modes to females.

The second concept, consensus, refers to the perceived number of people holding the same explanation of causality. Socialization of new officers involves acquainting them with the special qualities of the institution, which in many cases involves descriptions of the inmates incarcerated in that institution. Women inmates are likely to be described in terms which include characteristics and behavior patterns mentioned by our respondents. In other words, an officer entering a female facility and encountering difficulty may find ready agreement for the explanation that women behave differently from men and are more difficult to manage. Likewise, they may develop expectations of behavior from this indoctrination.

The concept of consistency involves the stability of observed behavior over time and place. Most of the officers interviewed had observed women in only one facility, but they often had accumulated experience in more than one male facility. This may result in either more or less willingness to generalize about male and female behavior. Looking at the results of the adjective checklist in Tables 5 and 6, it is clear that officers are more willing to generalize about female inmates (since a large amount of agreement was reached on a greater number of adjectives), even though their experience with them was typically limited to one facility.

Given high levels of consistency, consensus, and distinctiveness, it would be likely that officers would attribute the women's behavior to the characteristics of the group, i.e., to attributes of women as a group, rather than to the situation, i.e., to being in prison or under prison supervision. A key question is whether the "group" at issue is female in general or "female inmates" in particular. We saw evidence in the results of the adjective checklist exercise (see ch. 3) that there was probably a female stereotype operating which influenced the degree of consensus we measured for several adjectives. We can compare our finding to those adjectives that appear in a general stereotype of females as documented by social psychological literature. According to this literature a female stereotype incorporates such descriptive

traits as weak, helpless, nonathletic, domestic, maternal, inex-
perienced, seductive, flirtatious, emotional, sentimental, expressive, compassionate, nervous, scatterbrained, frivolous, shallow,
intuitive, perceptive, sensitive, humanistic, petty, gossipy, catty,
dependent, responsive, self-conscious, sweet, vain, tender, af-
fectionate, not aggressive, crying, inconsistent, quiet, passive,
and innocent. Men, on the other hand, would be described as
virile, strong, sloppy, brave, provider, aggressive, unemotional,
stoic, logical, rational, objective, scientific, practical, leader, dom-
inating, independent, individualistic, demanding, ambitious,
proud, egotistical, trustworthy, decisive, competitive, and adventurous.[5] We see that only some of the female personality traits
mentioned by the officers are represented in the above list. The
adjectives "emotional," "crying," "expressive," "inconsistent,"
"sensitive," "petty," and "dependent," are those which can be
found in the officers' responses. Several adjectives in the more
general stereotype are inconsistent with the officers' descriptions
of women's traits, such as "weak," "helpless," "dainty," "shy,"
"patient," "sweet," "tender," "not aggressive," "quiet," and
"passive."

It appears likely that officers hold a stereotype specific to female inmates. Studies have shown specific sex-linked stereotypes
in other settings. For instance, in schools and colleges, "good
students" are seen as calm, cooperative, dependable, obliging,
thorough, and mannerly only if they are female. Whereas "good"
male students are perceived as active, aggressive, assertive, independent, and curious.[6]

As noted in chapter 1, studies done in the workplace indicate
that managers may hold stereotyped views of women workers;
for example, females are only working for "pin" money; no one
wants a woman boss; women don't want the responsibility en-
tailed in many high-status jobs; women aren't worth hiring where
any training or investment is involved, since they just get married
or pregnant and quit; women are weak and frequently sick, and
they miss too many days of work; and women lack the physical
strength for many highly skilled and well-paid manual jobs, especially in the crafts.[7]

Another study found that females were believed to lack the
traits (leadership ability, competitiveness, self-confidence, objec-

tivity, aggressivity, forcefulness, ambitiousness, and responsibility) necessary to become successful managers. The female stereotype, by implication, would be one incorporating the opposites of these "managerial" traits.[8]

Broverman and Broverman, found that mental health practitioners held a stereotype of females (not necessarily of female patients) as more submissive than males, less independent, less adventurous, easily influenced, less aggressive, less competitive, more excitable in minor crises, more easily hurt, more emotional, less objective, and more conceited about their appearance. These traits, coincidentally, were also traits thought to be descriptive of a mentally unhealthy person.[9]

In examining the descriptions of females in other settings, it may be plausible that situationally specific stereotypes exist which involve those behavior and personality characteristics relevant to coping with that setting. One might also discover that behavior may surface which may well be inconsistent with the general female stereotype. For instance, we saw that almost 50 percent of the officers perceived women as more assaultive than men, a perception that is clearly at odds with the general female stereotype of nonaggressivity. This finding may suggest that women feel more at liberty to act assaultively in prison or that assaultiveness is necessary coping behavior in prison. Alternatively, it may be due to the opportunity of the officers to observe women in a confined setting. These observations may uncover assaultive behavior which is then compared to an "ideal" of what women should be like, and the result is a perception that women in prison are very assaultive.

Apparently, officers themselves did not sense any divergence between their perception of women in prison and women in general. When asked why the perceived differences exist, their responses included such phrases as "men are men and women are women," or "women are women whether they're in prison or not." Table 8 shows that officers clearly favor person or group attribution as explanations for perceived differences in male and female behavior rather than resorting to a situation-attribution explanation. Only 30 percent of the officers cited situational factors to account for the women's behavior. These officers pointed to differences in rule enforcement patterns or appli-

Table 8
**Officers' Causal Attributions of the Differences Perceived Between
Male and Female Inmates**

```
Behavior Attributed to:

   Institutional influences        28% (13)

   Individual differences          62% (28)

      --socialization differences  (10)
      --biological differences      (2)
      --undifferentiated           (16)

   Don't know, Other               10% ( 4)

                                    (N=45)
```

cations of sanctions as partially responsible for troublesome behavior from women.

Since officers were more likely to explain women's behavior
in terms of sex differences (whether biological or socialization)
rather than institutional factors, their response to inmate behavior is more likely to be an adaptation to the behavior rather
than an attempt to influence it. The inmates' behavior, in other
words, is taken for granted, and the officers see themselves as
doing their best within the confines of that assumption. Attempts
to change behavior by changing procedures, policies, or other
situational components are unlikely to be viewed as effective
since it is assumed that the behavior is not situationally induced.
We could, therefore, expect the officers to view inmate-gener-
ated problems with exasperated resignation, which indeed, appears to be their attitude.

IMPLICATIONS FOR MANAGEMENT

In this section we will compare the perceived differences of
male and female inmate behavior to hypothesized inmate subcultures. The standard descriptions of the male inmate subculture include the basic tenets of "do your own time," "don't rat,"
"don't talk to the man," and so on. This depiction characterizes
the inmate group as unified against an officer group, but it also
describes an atomized existence for the male inmate since be-

coming involved with each other's troubles is discouraged.[9] The women's prison is described in very different terms. Women in prison do not, according to published studies, follow the basic tenets of the male inmate code. Nor do female inmates presumably possess the loyalty to the inmate group that men do. Female inmates are ascribed emotional attachments to each other, often in the form of pseudofamily relationships, homosexual liaisons or very close friendships. It seems clear from previous studies, and also from our study, that in prison, men group together and can be managed through large groups, while women tend to form smaller cliques.[10]

This cumulative picture has several implications for prison management. In one sense, large groups are easier to deal with in that one has to communicate with fewer groups and leaders, and there is not the emotional component often present in the dyadic or triadic relationship. On the other hand, with larger formal groups, there is a greater potential for serious conflict, mass violence and organized resistence, since such groups can command the obedience of large numbers of inmates. Because of these reasons, male inmate protests may be taken more seriously.

Another subcultural difference which has been mentioned in the literature is the lack of group loyalty among women, manifested by jealousy, distrust, and deceit. It may be that the different patterning of female social groups promotes destructive as well as constructive relationships. For instance, with smaller groups and more personal ties observed among inmates in the female institution, there is a greater likelihood of conflicts occurring between these pairings. When officers say that women do not belong to larger inmate groups or that they feel no responsibility towards each other, it may be that this occurs because there is less to feel loyal to; instead of to an inmate membership group, one is loyal to one's friend or lover and no one else. Thus, the perception of disloyalty may be an unfair comparison of a difference between male and female reference groups which are the objects of loyalty.

Differences in social groupings would shape the communication patterns which are present in male and female prisons. A hierarchical "pyramid" pattern may be more descriptive of male prisons than of prisons for women. The closest one might come to an organized aggregation of female inmates is the kinship group with its shifting parental roles. This may very well be the reason for the perceived pettiness and personal nature of women's complaints, since there is no inmate authority body to sift complaints before presentation to administration.

Relationships between officers and inmates in women's prisons are more personal and are likely to be emotionally charged, unlike those normally found in prisons for men. There do not seem to be powerful subcultural norms against interaction with officers. These officer-inmate interactions tend to change and complicate the dynamics of a women's prison. There seems to be more involvement, and along with that involvement comes more potential for conflict.

Two other components of prison subculture are homosexuality and violence. In both, the male involvement can be described as covert, private, and "cold blooded." In women's prisons, homosexual activities and conflicts have been described as open, shared, and emotional. Implications for supervision are clear; whether or not one approves or disapproves of a behavior, it is much easier to ignore it if it is not visible. In the female facility, officers find it extremely difficult to ignore inmate behavior because there is less concealment. This may be the reason why homosexuality is considered more of a problem in prisons for women; and it may be why the officers who did perceive women to be more assaultive towards inmates did so, since inmate fights among women took place openly.

Another subcultural difference between prisons for men and women is the absence of norms against showing emotion (such as in the "real man" inmate role or in the general societal role of the stoic "he-man"). Among female inmates, the absence of the stoic norm makes it acceptable for the women to show a whole range of emotions, from love, affection, or friendship to sadness and anger towards other inmates or towards officers and administrators. This expressivity affects the management of women because the officer often must deal with an immediate open reaction to their interventions rather than a more suppressed one from the males. The open display of women's emotions resulted in many interpretations from the officers, i.e., lack of control, manipulation, moodiness, biological cycles, and so on. Whatever the interpretation, expressions of emotion did affect the officers' management style, in that officers had to be more concerned with anticipating how a woman was going to react to their actions or orders.

Another component of expressivity was the observed tendency among women to use self-destructiveness in an expressive way. Women in prison, it seems, frequently turn aggression towards themselves. In trying to understand this particular display of emotion, officers concluded that women sought attention from staff. The fact that women in prison succeed at suicide efforts much less frequently than men seems circumstantially to support the assumption that the inmates' actions have goals other than suicide.[11] Most generally, expressivity is relatively hard to respond to because the behavior is spontaneous, hence less predictable than behavior that is premeditated.

The literature on gender differences suggests that women and men perceive and respond to the world in different ways. One difference may be that women personalize relationships and events. We have already noted how relationships of female inmates with other inmates and staff tend to be more personal and to have more affective components than those of males. The officers also suggested that female inmates take the fact of incarceration more "personally" than males. This reaction seems to occur in response to disciplinary hearings and to officers giving orders and reprimands. Officers say that women "take things to heart" more than do males, which is another way of saying that the same event impacts more severely on the women. Women may not be able to isolate themselves from the impact of stress in the way that most men evidently can (or apparently can).

An orientation of women towards person rather than issue is partially implied by the alleged focus of women's demands and complaints. A perception that women are more selfish than men may be partially due to different care concerns of men and women. While women do seem to stick up for each other and be concerned for each other, this concern was focused on personal matters and took place spontaneously, whereas males were more often engaged in enterprises which were issue-oriented, planned, and organized.

To explore the causes of such perceived differences between male and female inmates, it may be useful to utilize the well-worn model of deprivation and importation. As we know from many previous studies, deprivation is the sum of problems posed by the institution or the incarceration experience which are thought to induce specific adaptations or responses; importation refers to different dispositions brought in from the outside by the inmates which affect their adaptation or response to the prison environment.[12]

Importation factors would include sex differences and the demographic differences of men and women inmates. Sex differences, as discussed before, might be biological, products of different socialization patterns, or a combination of the two. Officers perceive many sex differences (without regard to causation) between male and female inmates. The observed differences include more open and spontaneous displays of emotion and a more personalized approach to daily events and interactions. These "imported" differences, if they exist, may contribute to the difficulty officers experience when supervising women. For instance, officers describe a situation wherein both men and women may be upset about lack of movies, but women would tend to be more vocal and louder, and individually complain to anyone who is available, from the officer to the superintendent. Men, on the other hand, might grumble, but be less likely to spontaneously complain and more likely to go through channels, utilizing organized forms of resistance.

Another importation effect may relate to demographic differences between groups of men and women. Nationally, women inmates on the average, are older than the male inmate population. Also, women tend to have less extensive institutional experience than males. In our study, we collected little information on the demographic profile of the inmate populations, but we do know that in one representative state women had less extensive institutional experience (28% of incarcerated women had no prior criminal record as compared to 11% of men; and 55% of the males had prior institutional experience as compared to only 26% of the women). Also, in this state on the average, incarcerated women were older than the incarcerated male population.[13]

Lack of institutional experience may be one reason why women have more difficulty following prison rules. Officers mentioned that men seemed to be more "institutionalized" than women. The perception of some officers that women's behavior was similar to that of young males tends to support the idea that previous levels of institutionalization of men and women may be a partial reason for the different behavior patterns that the officers observed.

Deprivation factors would include institutional restrictions and the type of supervision received. Again, gender-related differences in the inmates' perceptions of the institutional experience would be important. We recall that the total prison experience is alleged to be more problematic for women than for men. Living situations, orders, separation from family—everything combines to make the experience more traumatic (at least according to our officers). This perception seems to be held in common by both women inmates and officers. Whether it is in fact true is hard to say. Ward and Kassebaum and Giallombardo wrestled with the question of whether prison was more of a deprivation for men or women, and both studies reached the conclusion that different aspects of imprisonment make up the deprivation experience for the two sexes.[14]

We have noted that institutions for women fall further along the treatment end of the treatment-custody continuum. The physical facility may be less harsh, the population smaller, and individualized attention seems to be the standard. In such settings, inmate subcultural norms tend to break down, especially the norms against interaction with staff or against personal involvements among inmates. Since very pronounced differences were observed by the officers, it may be that the type of institution is a critical variable of which the officers are relatively unaware. Some evidence of the institution's influence on behavior is found in the interviews with co-correctional officers, who tended to see less extreme behavioral differences between men and women inmates. Co-correctional officers were less likely than officers in single-sex facilities to believe that women were harder to supervise or that there were differences in supervising them.

Do officers in co-correctional institutions accurately perceive less extreme differences between male and female inmates? Or does the co-correctional institution, by its very nature, demand similar treatment and supervision of men and women inmates, which, in turn, elicit similar behavior? The effect that the type of institution has on behavior is not clear, but management and supervision style do seem to be factors one must add to the effect of imported sex differences.

One aspect of institutional differences involves the treatment of inmates by officers. In the women's institution, there seems to be more staff-inmate involvement,[15] which may circumvent inmate solidarity and subcultural norms, but may also tend to disrupt the smooth running of the facility, because authority is weakened by decreasing the social distance between inmates and officers. The reason this style of supervision is more likely to be found in women's facilities is partly due to the greater number of female correctional officers there who favor this style of supervision, but also a perception by both male and female officers that women are more in need of nurturance and personal support.

As with the perception that women find prison harder to endure, the perception that females need to be treated with more individualized attention, with more support and leniency, is shared by officers and inmates alike. At least this appears to be the case from the officers' descriptions of the inmates' behaviors and demands. Societal stereotypes of women being "softer" and "more emotional" seem to be shared by prison staff and no doubt influence their reactions to women in prison. It is also true that staff who feel that "prison is no place for a lady" may accept behavior which would be unacceptable to them from men.

Does behavior which is not suppressed continue to manifest itself and become a norm? Some officers hypothesized that women may be more openly aggressive in prison because there are no serious sanctions imposed against acting out. A woman in prison might be sent to segregation, but she would not be physically harmed, as she might by an opponent in a confrontation in free society. Thus, in prison, she has greater freedom to express emotions which she may have suppressed elsewhere, and she may be more likely to use physical force, a characteristic not represented among the gender norms of society. In prison, violence is more easily accepted and also serves as a deterrent to abuse from other inmates.

From the information we have presented, one can conclude

that both importation and deprivation factors may contribute to the perceived differences in the behaviors in prisons for males and females. The assumption that differences in supervision may affect the behavior of women needs to be tested more thoroughly, and co-correctional facilities may be the place to do so. Since male correctional officers seem to treat women inmates differently than do most female officers, this difference may also be a suitable area for study. Of course, it would be difficult to separate the effect of different supervision styles from the effect of opposite-sex officers, which is also an element in the perceived differences.

The style of supervision more commonly associated with female officers and more often found in female institutions seems to have both advantages and disadvantages. It personalizes interactions and may alleviate inmate isolation and alienation. Through these interviews, one becomes aware of how difficult it must be for men in prison, where one is unlikely to have close friends or be able to express affection or even grief or sadness, because men must suppress feelings "like a man" or fight it out "like a man." This syndrome clearly relates to the prevalence of completed suicides, suicide attempts, and more serious assaults in prisons for men.[16]

The empathetic supervison style may ease prison adjustment, but if carried to an extreme, it runs the risk of sacrificing authority and it may result in dangerous emotional confrontations. A formalistic style of supervision tends to result in greater fairness and predictability, but may exacerbate rather than diffuse potential conflicts. Women and men are perceived to have different needs for attention and support; thus, some supervision variation may be appropriate. However, some of the problems officers experience in supervising women may be partially due to the supervision style they have developed.

Correctional administrators should be able to use these findings in training new officers or officers who are transferred to prisons housing members of the opposite sex. For instance, exposure to these issues could be used as discussion aids. It is true that an expectation of sex differences may very well ensure that officers will perceive them. However, it may also be true that "forewarned is forearmed," and officers who are trained to expect changes in their own behavior may be able to control the negative consequences of such changes. For instance, avoid the loss of authority which results from emotional involvement.

Correctional managers may also take a cue from the last pages of our chapter on supervision regarding what types of people may enjoy working with women. It seems that those correctional officers who seek involvement and who have greater needs for challenge and excitement may be more suited to working with women than are officers who seek more stable and predictable job assignments. In order to avoid officer frustration, it may be possible to screen officers entering female facilities to ensure that those who work in them have these types of needs. It may be that there are male officers who would be very comfortable supervising women (the "human service officer" discussed in chapter 1 comes to mind) and, alternatively, some female officers may be more comfortable supervising males. Thus, one might be able to reduce stress for both types of officers by allowing them to be in the environment in which they would be most comfortable.

One additional point should be noted. It seems to be the case after analyzing these officer interviews that cross-sex supervision, despite its problems, has the potential to improve officer-inmate relations in both types of facilities. The "human service officer" finds new allies in women C.O.'s and male inmates profit from this attention and assistance. Alternatively, the more informal, "personal" relationships between female officers and inmates are scrutinized with the entry of male officers. Perhaps some amount of familiarity should be sacrificed to encourage unbiased treatment of inmates and recognition of female inmates as adults responsible for their behavior.

NOTES

1. F. Heider, *New Approaches to Social Problems* (San Francisco: Josey-Bass Publishers, 1979).

2. H. H. Kelley, "The Processes of Causal Attribution," *American Psychologist* 28 (1973): 107–128.

3. Kelley, "The Processes of Causal Attribution": 108.

4. Kelley, "The Processes of Causal Attribution": 112.

5. J. S. Chafetz, *Masculine, Feminine or Human* (Itasca, IL: Peacock Publishers, 1978), p. 38.

6. Chafetz, *Masculine, Feminine or Human*, p. 38.

7. V. Schein, "The Relationship Between Sex Role Stereotypes and Requisite Management Characteristics," *Journal of Applied Psychology* 57 (1973): 95–100.

8. I. K. Broverman and D. M. Broverman, "Sex Role Stereotypes and Clinical Judgments of Mental Health," *Journal of Consulting and Clinical Psychology* 34, 1 (1970): 59–78.

9. L. Bowker, *Prisoner Subcultures* (Lexington, MA: Lexington Books, 1977).

10. All of the concepts herein mentioned have been discussed previously in the text of this book.

11. J. Fox, "Women in Crisis," in *Men in Crisis* by Hans Toch (Chicago: Aldine Publishers, 1975).

12. For a discussion of these theories, see L. Bowker, *Prisoner Subcultures*.

13. D. McDonald and J. Grossman, "Analysis of Low Return Rate Among Female Offenders," New York Department of Correctional Services (unpublished document, 1981).

14. D. Ward and G. Kassebaum, *Women's Prison: Sex and Social Structure* (Chicago: Aldine Publishers, 1965); and R. Giallombardo, *The Social World of Imprisoned Girls* (New York: John Wiley and Sons, 1974).

15. It should be mentioned that these characteristics are also present in some minimum security and/or treatment-oriented prisons, with the same consequences for the inmate subculture. C. McEwen, "Subcultures in Community based Programs," in L. Ohlin, A. Miller, and R. Coates, *Juvenile Correctional Reform in Massachusetts* (Washington, D.C.: National Institute for Juvenile Justice, LEAA, 1972).

16. H. Toch, *Men in Crisis* (Chicago: Aldine Publishers, 1975).

7

Methodology

This research is exploratory. The number of interviews we reported on is not large (sixty) by most standards. What was more important than the number of interviews was the experiential richness of each interview. We prized the officer who was articulate and perceptive in describing the environment of the prison and the differences that he or she experienced. The decision to use a phenomenological approach was made because of the exploratory nature of the study and also because of the topic. Sex differences, even limited to observable behaviors, are difficult to document, much less explain. We have, therefore, limited this research to *perceptions* of sex differences. Although one might certainly use the perceptions presented here as a springboard for hypothesis testing, the observations of differences between the behavior of men and women should not be taken as verified data.

These observations, however, are important in their own right. It is well-known that beliefs and perceptions affect an individual's behavior; therefore, officers' perceptions of male and female inmates determine their behavior towards them, quite apart from the "objective reality" of male and female inmates' "true" behavior patterns. Female inmates, for example, may be more emotional than male inmates. Alternatively, if officers *perceive* and *believe* women to be more emotional, they will *act* in relation to women as if they were. In turn, the women may behave emotionally because they are more emotional, because they are responding to cues from officers, or because of some combination of factors.

Bias held by the observer may affect perceptions in two ways. The observer may be more likely to notice behavior when it fits into a preconceived stereotype of sex-typed behavior. This may also affect our officers' perceptions in the sense that they are observing women in a total environment. Hence, if they observe behavior that is outside the realm of their stereotype of what is appropriate for females, they may then perceive female inmates to be "different."

There may be factors other than the sex of the inmate which influence the observed behavioral and personality differences of men and women. One factor might be the type of institution and the effect it may have on the inmates housed there. One must also be aware that incarceration itself may be a factor, and that the behavior of men and women in prison may not be the same as one would find outside prison walls. A very important factor in the observed differences may be different treatment of men and women by officers. In this respect, a situation similar to a self-fulfilling prophecy may somehow operate; i.e., women may be treated as if they would react more emotionally, and because that expectation is somehow relayed to them through the officers' behavior, they may indeed become more emotional in reacting to daily events.

Interviews were the primary tool of data collection to gain insight into the officers' views regarding male and female inmates. The proportion of officers who differentiate inmates by gender in terms of management problems has never been established, so one objective was to develop a base of knowledge about the actual number of officers who believed women were more difficult to supervise, men were more difficult, or there were no differences between the two.

Although objective measurements of inmate-officer interactions would be useful, they would be extremely difficult to interpret. Official reports would reveal little about what officers themselves perceive as problematic and why. Neither would they show how the interactions between officers and inmates are influenced by the perceptions or preconceptions of the officers or how the inmates' behavior is shaped by the officers' handling of inmates based on these perceptions. Semistructured interviewing was selected as the methodology to be used because responses are relatively standardized and lend themselves to easy grouping and tabulations, but there is still the opportunity to stimulate free thought.

THE INTERVIEW

In our interview, we started by having the subject fill out an adjective checklist (see Appendix C), adapted from Gough's Adjective Checklist, to separately characterize male and female inmates. It was fairly easy for most individuals to go through the list, which was presented twice on one page, and to check adjectives on the first list which applied to males, and on the second list for females. The instructions given for this exercise emphasized that the officer was expected to generalize and use his or her first impressions.

The original list of adjectives was reduced by eliminating those which were infrequently or never checked by the preliminary interviewees. Thus, of the original seventy-five adjectives, only forty-eight were used for the correctional officer interviews.

The body of the interview consisted of primary and secondary probes in each of the three areas of inquiry (see Appendix B). The first area of questioning involved institutional differences between prisons for men and women. The officers were asked whether they had noted any general differences between male and female facilities. After the officer volunteered differences they regarded as noteworthy, a number of checklist attributes were presented to the officers, who were then asked whether they had noticed these as institutional differences. The suggested items included standard institutional attributes such as size, rules, procedures, and so on.

Next, the perceived differences between male and female inmates were explored. The officer was asked the question: "Now, can you tell me if you've observed any differences between male and female inmates? First, any dominant personality traits that seem to be present in either female inmates or male inmates?" The officers were reminded of the adjective checklist and asked to expand upon the adjectives they had checked for either sex.

If they combined several traits in one response, each point was resuscitated and explored separately. If the response was inappropriate, i.e., if it dealt with another area of questioning or was irrelevant, the information was recorded, and the officers were urged to expand on any personality differences they had observed (the interviewer stressed "personality" and/or "traits" to get the individuals back on the track). If it became apparent that the subjects did not understand, or that they had exhausted their observations, the researcher went on to the secondary probes. A number of traits were suggested, and the interviewees were asked whether those belonged to one sex or the other. The secondary probes were all phrased as "Have you found women inmates to be more (the trait) than male inmates?" or "Are either male inmates or female inmates more (the trait)?" The traits suggested in the secondary probes were compiled from a literature review and from informal discussions with correctional personnel. For instance, we have mentioned that many people have stated that women are more emotional, so that trait was included. Since studies have indicated that women may be more open with personal problems, that was another trait used.

Another area of questioning involved the differential needs of men and women, e.g., does either sex have a greater need for doctors or counselors? The overt behavior of men and women inmates was also explored. Again, lists of behaviors were compiled according to what was learned or might be inferred from previous studies and what had been picked up in early discussions and interviews. The officers were asked whether they had observed these behaviors to be more frequent among either men or women. The behaviors which were suggested to the respondents included assaultiveness, "acting out," drug use, following orders with or without argument, homosexual practices, and the tendency to form organized groups with leaders.

Another area of the interview covered perceived supervision problems. Responses to these queries often merely recapped and validated earlier responses. For instance, when speaking about individual differences, officers who had described women inmates as more argumentative also often mentioned that it took more effort to enforce rules with women because they would argue, whereas men would perform what was asked of them.

Various factors relating specifically to supervision were introduced at this point if they had not already been brought out, such as whether the officers felt greater danger from men or women, whether men or women were more unpredictable, had more problems, and were easier to get to know. The officers were also asked whom they preferred to supervise and why. They were asked directly whether women were harder to supervise and why. They were asked whether there were any situations where they would need to or should treat women and men differently. The final question involved a summing up of what respondents thought to be the major factors which resulted in supervision differences, and their causes.

An effort was made throughout the interview to give the subjects the opportunity to present their own observations, and only when they had finished speaking did the interviewer use the secondary probes. It was also decided not to interrupt the interviewees if they were answering another part of the interview, but rather to bring them back only after they had completed a line of thought. For this reason, the interviews were not always conducted in the order presented in the interview format.

The interviews were recorded on tape and transcribed when possible. (Only a few officers refused to be taped. In these cases, the interviewer took extensive notes.) All of the relevant quotes from the interviews were then collated for each question and subject matter category. Content analysis was used to identify themes or subareas of the responses. For instance, many of the personality traits mentioned involved several components which were brought out by different interviewees. While many officers agreed, for instance, that women were more "emotional," it was clear that this conclusion was not based on a consistent or unanimous perception of "emotionality." Some officers used emotionality to describe behavior, e.g., acting out, crying, and so on, while others were referring to less tangible attributes, such as a greater need for affiliation or a greater sensitivity to events or people.

The officers were encouraged to include examples and descriptions of behavior in each response, and this information has been used to elaborate the findings. The steps used for analysis were as follows. First, the interviews were played back, and discrete (yes/no) responses were recorded on the questionnaire forms. The interview responses were also transcribed and attached to the questionnaire. Then, for each question, the yes/ no response from each interview was recorded along with the relevant quotes wherever they appeared in the interview. The findings at this point were grouped according to question answered, i.e., all sixty responses to the first question, the second question and all the responses to it; and so on. The yes/no responses were then tabulated and percentages of agreement were arrived at. In a few cases, the discrete yes/no answers were not capable of capturing the responses of the officers; for instance, to the question "Are women in prison more masculine than women on the outside?" Some officers said yes or no, but most said "some" referring to those women who choose the masculine ("stud") role in the inmate subculture.

The next step involved content analysis of the transcribed descriptive answers. Sometimes there was not a great deal to work with because the question did not provoke much interest or seemed to have little relevance for the officer. In many cases, however, the responses were extremely lengthy, with many examples and/or components. In these cases, it was necessary to separate the individual themes and explore these in the findings section.

SUBJECTS

The preliminary phase of the interviewing process involved speaking with fifteen key people in correctional facilities and in the central office of the state department of corrections. These individuals were identified and chosen based on either their work experience in male and female facilities and/or their location in the system (i.e., as a top administrator of a facility which employed a large number of officers who would be interviewed). The interviews conducted with these fifteen people helped clarify issues and improved the format used for the interviews with correctional officers. Table 10 describes the individuals interviewed during this phase of the research.

As one can see from the table, our preliminary interviews were done with individuals who, on the average, had over ten years

Table 9
Profile of Subjects Used for Preliminary Interviews

Average Number of Year
Spent Working with:

Sex of Interviewee	Women Inmates	Male Inmates
Male (n=8)	3.5	7.4
Female (n=7)	6.8	5.7

Current Position:	
administrative/Central	6
administrative/facility	5
nurse	1
educational supervisor	1
psychologist	1
senior counselor	1

of experience in the state correctional system. Almost evenly divided between male and female, these individuals were from a variety of work backgrounds, although most held administrative positions at the time of the interview. As would be expected, the female interviewees had more years of experience with female inmates, while the males had more experience with male inmates.

The main body of interviews was conducted with forty-five experienced correctional officers (and a few sergeants). To select these subjects, the names of all correctional officers who had

Table 10
Profile of Correctional Officers Interviewed

Number of Years the Officer had Worked With:

Sex of Office Interviewed	Female Inmates		Male Inmates	
	1-5 Yrs.	5+ Yrs.	1-5 Yrs.	5+ Yrs.
Female (n=18)	28% (5)	72% (13)	50% (9)	50% (9)
Male (n=27)	82% (22)	19%[*] (5)	30% (8)	70% (19)

[*]Percentages may not add up to 100% because of rounding.

Table 11
Work Experience of Correctional Officers in the Sample
(Type of Facility)

	Female C.O.'s		Male C.O.'s	
Type of Facility	Female C.F.	Male C.F.	Female C.F.	Male C.F.
Minimum/Medium	67%* (12)	17% (3)	48% (13)	19% (5)
Maximum	17% (3)	50% (9)	52% (14)	30% (8)
Both types	71% (3)	33% (6)	0% (0)	52% (14)
	(n=18)	(n=18)	(n=27)	(n=27)

*Percentages may not add up to 100% because of rounding.

worked for at least one year in a facility for men and at least
one year in a facility for women were recorded from the employee records of the department. Lists were made identifying
where these officers were located, and those facilities which employed the greatest numbers of these selected officers were con-
tacted and interviews were requested. Approval was obtained
from the agency's central office and cooperation was garnered
at each facility in arranging the time and location of the interviews with the officers. Officers indicated their willingness to
participate by signing a letter of consent which explained the
purpose of the interviews and requested their assistance. From
an initial pool of 100 officers, interviews were completed with
45 who met the criteria.

Officers who were interviewed had appreciable experience in
both male and female (or co-correctional) facilities. Female correctional officers were more likely than male correctional officers
to have had cross-sex inmate supervision experience. Fifty percent of the women had five or more years of experience in a
male institution, while only 19 percent of the men had five or
more years of experience in a female (or co-correctional) facility.
Roughly 70 percent of both men and women had five years or
more involvement in an institution housing members of their
own sex, so our sample is composed of fairly experienced officers. Table 11 shows that female officers were more likely to
have worked under varying levels of security for both sexes,

while male officers were more likely to have had experience with varying levels of security for males, but tended to have more specialized experience dealing with females. This is the case because there are fewer facilities for women, and thus the officers did not have the opportunity to work in a number of custody settings.

RELIABILITY AND VALIDITY

Reliability in this case refers to the replicability of our findings. In other words, how likely it is our findings will be reproduced in any future study. Our method of testing reliability is checking response agreement with an independent rater. Even though our study is only exploratory, it is important to determine whether our findings could be replicated by another researcher. The major part of the study relies on the percentages of officer agreements in the discrete responses to the secondary probes, as described previously. We may assume there is a high probability that these responses might be replicated since we polled roughly one-half of the "population" and discrete responses are not subject to individual interpretation. In some areas of the discussion, however, we use content analysis of officers' responses to isolate and identify themes. The identification of these themes does involve a subjective judgment on the part of the rater, and so a reliability check of this material is very important.

We used an independent rater to determine whether the themes identified by the author could be recognized by another person. In the responses of the officers to the initial probe about differences between male and female inmates, content analysis was used to uncover three themes; women were described as more defiant, as exhibiting open displays of emotion, and as gratification-seeking.

The theme of defiance is defined as argumentativeness, refusing to follow orders, being "harder to handle," likely to question orders, confrontational, critical, and lacking respect. The theme of exhibiting open displays of emotion involved visible behavior stemming from emotions or feelings, such as crying, screaming, throwing tantrums, being noisy, being more explosive, and losing one's temper. The last theme of gratification seeking included responses which described women as needing more affection, more attention, more sympathy; being more dependent; and also wanting things, demanding more, being less patient, and wanting things "right now."

These three themes were explained to the independent rater, and then the rater read a sample of twenty responses and indicated whether each theme appeared or did not appear in each response. The author went through the same procedure, and percentages of inter-rater agreements were computed by dividing the total number of responses into the number of agreements. For each of these themes, rater responses agreed 75 percent of the time.

Content analysis was also used in analyzing the correctional officers' descriptions of emotionality. Three themes emerged in these responses: "open displays of emotion," "need for affectional ties," and "moodiness." The same procedure as described above was followed with an independent rater and a sample of twenty responses. there was 90 percent inter-rater agreement for the theme involving open displays of emotion; 85 percent agreement for the theme "need for affectional ties"; and agreement reached 90 percent for the theme of moodiness.

Validity refers to the degree of confidence one has as to whether the study has measured what was intended. This is usually checked by using several methods to measure the same thing. We can test the validity of our descriptive interview responses against the discrete (yes/no) responses which provides a reliability check (to make sure the officer can substantiate his answer with experiences and, therefore, will most likely give the same answer if asked the same question at a later time), and also a validity check (since the question itself with the response of the officer is separate from the officer's description of that adjective and can be compared to make sure the officer means the same thing as the interviewer when referring to the adjective).

With respect to our sample, our claim is only that we have measured and can present the perceptions of correctional officers who have worked with both male and female inmates. Since we have included a large percentage of the total universe of officers who have worked with both sexes for over one year or longer (almost 50 percent), it seems safe to assume that our sample is not biased even though it was obtained by selection rather than by random sampling.

The reason we make no claim that our findings are valid for other state systems is because of the bias which influences officers' perceptions when a single facility or a single system is involved. To illustrate, let us assume that an officer has worked in several male facilities, each with different superintendents, different geographic locations, different demographics of staff, and different procedures. The officer would be able to generalize about "male" institutions by bringing out similarities between facilities as representative of male facilities. This is not possible with female facilities since the officer is apt to have had experience in only one female facility. Thus, if it happens to be a chaotic facility with haphazard rule enforcement, the officer may very well assume that all female facilities possess these characteristics. Although we may be able to generalize our findings regarding officer perceptions of male facilities from this state to other states, we would be less likely to do so with any confidence for our data describing officers' experiences with the few female facilities involved.

The major thrust of this work was exploratory. Now that the preliminary questions have been answered, more in-depth studies must follow to test some of the propositions presented in this book.

APPENDIX A

Comparison of Officers'
Perceptions with Findings of
Previous Studies

AUTHOR(S) OF STUDY	FINDING OF STUDY	PERCEPTIONS AGREE?
DIFFERENTIAL INSTITUTIONAL CHARACTERISTICS:		
Ward and Kassebaum, Heffernan, Rotner	architectural differences between institutions for men and women	YES
Wheeler	depersonalized atmosphere not present in smaller institutions	YES
Baunach and Murton, Ardeti	lack of programs in prisons for women	NO
Potter, Griffith, Moyer	different perceptions of "clients" (men and women)	YES
Zingraff, Lindquist	different control patterns and rule enforcement	YES
Street, Vinter and Perrow, Cressey, Zald	individualized treatment program and delivery results in staff dis- content and conflict	YES

OTHER DIFFERENCES:

Haley, Baunach, McGowan, Palmer	women have more problems due to children and family	YES
Feinman, Eyman	women have greater need for medical services and counseling services	YES NO
Weitman	women exhibit more conforming attitudes in prison	NO
Kay	women exhibit more negative attitudes in prison	YES
Burkhart, Ardeti	staff in women's prisons tend to treat inmates like children	YES
Potter	women seem to need more care	YES

Appendix A (*continued*)

AUTHOR(S) OF STUDY	FINDING OF STUDY	PERCEPTIONS AGREE?
SUPERVISION DIFFERENCES:		
Kissel and Seidel, Potter, Zimmer, Ackerman	male and female correctional officers perform their jobs in different styles	YES
BEHAVIOR DIFFERENCES:		
Lindquist	more assaults among women	YES
McKerracher, Street and Segal	more acting out types of behavior among women	MIXED
Lombroso, Thomas, Pollak, Knopka	women in prison more masculine	MIXED (Some)
Giallombardo, Tittle, Ward and Kassebaum	different needs fulfilled by male and female homosexuality, also manifested differently	YES

Van de Wormer	masculinity related to homosexual involvement	YES
Fox	different causes for suicidal behavior of men and women	YES

PRISON SOCIAL ORGANIZATION AND RELATIONSHIPS:

Tittle, Sharf and Hickey	differences in social organization	YES
Zingraff, Kruttschnitt, Jensen, Sieverdes and Bartollas	differences in adherences to "inmate subculture" between men and women	YES

GENDER-LINKED PERSONALITY TRAITS AMONG INMATES:

Eysenck	higher psychoticism scores for women (with resulting behavior differences)	MIXED
Panton	Males score higher on: complaining	NO
	Females score higher on: withdrawal from social intercourse	NO
	sensitivity	YES

143

Appendix A (*continued*)

AUTHOR(S) OF STUDY	FINDING OF STUDY	PERCEPTIONS AGREE?
Joesting et al.	Males score higher on:	
	submissiveness to authority	YES
	hypochondria	NO
	introversion	YES
	Females score higher on:	
	hostile response	YES
	conforming attitude	NO
Widom	No difference in self-esteem	YES

APPENDIX B

Sample of Interview
Questionnaire

M   F
___ ___

INSTITUTIONAL DIFFERENCES

Are there differences in the facilities for men and women, either physically or the way the institution is run? How does it affect supervision?

Affect?

Secondary probes: Any differences?   Affects Supervision?

Security measures _____

Size _____

Rules and Regs _____

Loosely run _____

Familiarity _____
....

INDIVIDUAL DIFFERENCES:

Now can you tell me if you've observed any differences between male and female inmates. First, any personality traits that seem to be present in either female inmates or male inmates.

Trait: Examples:

_____

_____

_____

_____

_____

_____

_____

_____

_____

147

Appendix B (*continued*)

Secondary Probes:

Examples:

demanding   YES   NO   _____

emotional   YES   NO   _____

complaining   YES   NO   _____

assertive   YES   NO   _____

irresponsible   YES   NO   _____

openness   YES   NO   _____

honest   YES   NO   _____

SUPERVISION DIFFERENCES

This last section deals with any differences you have to make in supervising men and women.

First of all, do you have a preference?   M   F   _____

How about if you were a counselor?   M   F   _____

Are women more difficult to supervise?   Y   N   _____

Are there any differences in supervising?   Y   N   _____

Different problems of inmates?   Y   N   _____

Dangerousness differences?   Y   N   _____

Unpredictable differences?   Y   N   _____

Easier to get to know?   Y   N   _____

Are there any situations where you would have to treat women and men differently?   Y   N

Appendix B (*continued*)

Which of the characteristics, either institutional or individual, do you think are the most important in making supervision different?

Why do you think these differences exist?

APPENDIX C

Sample of Adjective Checklist

DIRECTIONS: Please think back over your experiences with inmates and check off the adjectives that apply. In the first section check off adjectives which apply to male inmates and in the second section adjectives which apply to female inmates. Work quickly and use the first impression that comes to mind.

MALE:

active ___	confident ___	headstrong ___	noisy ___
aggressive ___	considerate ___	high-strung ___	quarrelsome ___
aloof ___	cruel ___	honest ___	rebellious ___
anxious ___	cynical ___	hostile ___	self-centered ___
argumentative ___	deceitful ___	immature ___	self-punishing ___
arrogant ___	defensive ___	impulsive ___	sensitive ___
assertive ___	demanding ___	irresponsible ___	stubborn ___
boastful ___	dependent ___	irritable ___	suspicious ___
bossy ___	distrustful ___	kind ___	temperamental ___
capable ___	emotional ___	lazy ___	touchy ___
changeable ___	evasive ___	manipulative ___	tough ___
complaining ___	excitable ___	moody ___	vindictive ___

FEMALE

active ___	confident ___
aggressive ___	considerate ___
aloof ___	cruel ___
anxious ___	cynical ___
argumentative ___	deceitful ___
arrogant ___	defensive ___
assertive ___	demanding ___
boastful ___	dependent ___
bossy ___	distrustful ___
capable ___	emotional ___
changeable ___	evasive ___
complaining ___	excitable ___

headstrong ___	noisy ___
high-strung ___	quarrelsome ___
honest ___	rebellious ___
hostile ___	self-centered ___
immature ___	self-punishing ___
impulsive ___	sensitive ___
irresponsible ___	stubborn ___
irritable ___	suspicious ___
kind ___	temperamental ___
lazy ___	touchy ___
manipulative ___	tough ___
moody ___	vindictive ___

- -

DO NOT WRITE IN THIS SPACE

M   F

||	||
||	||

153

Selected Bibliography

Ardeti, R. "The Sexual Segregation of American Prisons." *Yale Law Journal* 82 (1973): 1229–73.

Block, P., and D. Anderson. *Policewomen on Patrol.* Washington, D.C.: Police Foundation, 1974.

Bowker, L. *Women and Crime in America.* New York: Macmillan Publishing Co., 1981.

———. *Prison Victimization.* New York: Elsevier, 1980.

———. *Women, Crime and the Criminal Justice System.* Lexington, MA: Lexington Books, 1978.

Chafetz, J. S. *Masculine, Feminine or Human.* Itasca, IL: Peacock Press, 1978.

Chapman, J. *Women Employed in Corrections.* Washington, D.C.: National Institute of Justice, 1983.

Crouch, B., ed. *The Keepers: Prison Guards and Contemporary Corrections.* Springfield, IL: Charles C. Thomas, 1980.

Eyman, J. *Prison for Women: A Practical Guide to Administrative Problems.* Springfield, IL: Charles C. Thomas, 1971.

Feinman, C. *Women in the Criminal Justice System.* New York: Praeger Publishers, 1980.

Freedman, E. "Their Sister's Keepers: A Historical Perspective of Female Correctional Institutions in the U.S." *Feminist Studies* 2 (1974): 77–95.

General Accounting Office. *Female Offenders: Who Are They and What Are the Problems Confronting Them?* Washington, D.C.: Government Printing Office, 1979.

Giallombardo, R. *Society of Women.* New York: John Wiley, 1966.

Hazelrigg, L., ed. *Prison Within Society.* Garden City, N.Y.: Doubleday, 1968.

Heffernan, R. *The Square, the Cool and the Life.* New York: John Wiley and Sons, 1972.

Horne, P. *Women in Law Enforcement.* Springfield, IL: Charles C. Thomas, 1975.

Johnson, R. and S. Price. "The Complete Correctional Officer: Human Service and the Human Environment of Prison." *Criminal Justice and Behavior* 8, no. 3 (1981): 343–73.

Kissel, P. and J. Seidel. *The Management and Impact of Female Corrections Officers at Jail Facilities Housing Male Inmates.* Boulder, Co: National Institute of Corrections, 1980.

Lekkerkerker, E. C. *Reformatories for Women in the U.S.* Gronigen, Netherlands: J. B. Wolters, 1931.

Lindquist, C. "Prison Discipline and the Female Offender." *Journal of Offender Counseling, Services and Rehabilitation* 4, no. 4 (1980): 305–319.

Maccoby, E. and C. N. Jacklin, *The Psychology of Sex Differences.* Stanford, CA: Stanford University Press, 1974.

McKerracher, D. W., D.R.K. Street and L. S. Segal. "A Comparison of the Behavior Problems Presented by Male and Female Subnormal Offenders." *British Journal of Psychiatry* 112 (1966): 891–99.

Martin, S. *Breaking and Entering: Policewomen on Patrol.* Berkeley, CA: University of California Press, 1980.

———. "POLICEwoman and PoliceWOMAN: Occupational Role Dilemmas and Choices of Female Officers." *Journal of Police Science and Administration* 7, no. 3 (1979): 314–23.

Mitchell, A. *Informal Inmate Social Structure in Prisons for Women: A Comparative Study.* San Francisco: R & E Research Associates, 1975.

Potter, J. "In Prison, Women Are Different." *Corrections Magazine* 4, no. 4 (1978): 14–24.

———. "Should Women Guards Work in Prisons for Men?" *Corrections Magazine* 6, no. 5 (1980), 30–38.

Price, B. and N. Sokoloff. *The Criminal Justice System and Women.* New York: Clark Boardman and Company, 1982.

Remmington, P. *Policing—The Occupation and the Introduction of Female Officers—An Anthropologist's Study.* Lanham, MD: University Press of America, 1981.

Ross, R. ed. *Prison Guard/Correctional Officer.* Toronto: Butterworths, 1981.

Ruback, B. "The Sexually Integrated Prison—A Legal and Policy Evaluation." *American Journal of Criminal Law* 3 (1975): 310–30.

Simon, R. *Women and Crime.* Lexington, MA: D. C. Heath and Co., 1975.

Smart, C. *Women, Crime and Criminology: A Feminist Critique.* London: Routledge and Kegan Paul, 1976.

Smith, A. *Women In Prison: A Study in Penal Methods.* London: Stevens
    Publishers, 1962.
Smykla, J. *Co-Corrections: A Case Study of a Coed Federal Prison.* Wash-
    ington, D.C.: University Press of America, 1978.
Tittle, C. "Inmate Organization: Sex Differentiation and the Influence
    of Criminal Subcultures." *American Sociological Review* 34 (1969):
    492–505.
Ward, D. and G. Kassebaum. *Women's Prison: Sex and Social Structure.*
    Chicago: Aldine Publishers, 1965.
Warren, M., ed. *Comparing Female and Male Offenders.* Beverly Hills, CA:
    Sage Publications, 1981.
Zingraff, M. "Inmate Assimilation: A Comparison of Male and Female
    Delinquents." *Criminal Justice and Behavior* 7, no. 3 (1980): 275–
    92.

Index

About the Author

JOYCELYN M. POLLOCK, Assistant Professor of Criminal Justice, University of Houston-Downtown, has done research in the areas of corrections and women in criminal justice. Her published works include "Early Theories in Female Criminality" in Lee Bowker, *Women, Crime and the Criminal Justice System,* and "Women Will Be Women: Correctional Officers' Perceptions of the Emotionality of Women Inmates" in *Prison Journal.*